Weight Loss Recipes

-no sugar, no flour, made deliciously easy-

Volume 8

Weight Loss Recipes
- no sugar, no flour, made deliciously easy -
WeightLossRecipesCookbook.com

Books by Natalie Aul

1. Weight Loss Recipes Cookbook **Volume 1**
2. Weight Loss Recipes Cookbook **Volume 2**
3. Weight Loss Recipes Cookbook **Volume 3**
4. Weight Loss Recipes Cookbook **Volume 4**
5. Weight Loss Recipes Cookbook **Volume 5**
6. Weight Loss Recipes Cookbook **Volume 6**
7. Weight Loss Recipes Cookbook **Volume 7**
8. Weight Loss Recipes Cookbook **Volume 8**
9. Cooking with Joy
10. Weight Loss Recipes Cookbook **Whole Food, Plant Based, & Vegan Volume**
11. Simply Delicious **A 14 Day Food Plan**

Copyright © 2020 by Natalie Aul

All rights reserved. No part of this publication may be reproduced, stored in a retrieval system, or transmitted by any means – electronic, mechanical, photocopying, recording, or otherwise – without prior written permission from the author. The only exception is for the furtherance of the Gospel of salvation, or brief quotations in printed reviews.

Scripture quotations are from the King James Version of the Bible if not otherwise indicated.

Scripture quotations marked TPT are from The Passion Translation®. Copyright © 2017, 2018 by Passion & Fire Ministries, Inc. Used by permission. All rights reserved. ThePassionTranslation.com. All Scripture quotations are from The Passion Translation®. Copyright © 2017, 2018 by Passion & Fire Ministries, Inc. Used by permission. All rights reserved. ThePassionTranslation.com.

"Scripture quotations taken from the Amplified® Bible (AMP), Copyright © 2015 by The Lockman Foundation Used by permission. www.Lockman.org"

"Scripture quotations taken from the Amplified® Bible (AMPC), Copyright © 1954, 1958, 1962, 1964, 1965, 1987 by The Lockman Foundation Used by permission. www.Lockman.org"

Scripture taken from The Message. Copyright Â© 1993, 1994, 1995, 1996, 2000, 2001, 2002. Used by permission of NavPress Publishing Group.

Digital images from digitalstampdesign.blogspot.com

Printed in the United States of America

ISBN

Special Thanks to:

My sister Kelly, without you this book would not be possible!

My mom Maggie, for your encouragement, and introducing us to this new way of life.

To everyone who has sent me encouraging notes and such lovely reviews of my other cookbook volumes, you have all been so sweet!

I give all the glory to God, without Him I can do nothing.

Contents

Breakfast

Page

12 7 Layer Banana Split

14 Applelicious Chia Bars

16 Baked Pumpkin Rice Crispy Bar

18 Beans and Rice Waffle

20 Blueberry Cobbler Oatmeal

22 Blueberry Lemon Parfait

24 Blueberry Peach Crumble

26 Breakfast Cheesecake with Oatmeal Crust

28 Dreamy Creamy Tahini Oatmeal

30 Crunch Berry Parfait

32 Blueberry Roasted Pear Crunch Bowl

34 Blueberry Lemon Chia Pudding

36 Fruity Limesicle Parfait

38 Mango Toast

40 Monkey Chia Pudding

42 Morning Glory Donuts

44 Peanut Butter Ricotta Apple Spice Bowl

46 Pizza Rice Waffle

48 Pumpkin Apple Waffles

50 Pumpkin Rice Crispy Bar

52 Roasted Pear Raspberry Oatmeal

54 Strawberry Shortcake Chia Pudding

56 Toasted Sweet Potato and Almond Butter Bowl

58 Vanilla Sponge Cake

60 Blueberry Lemon Breakfast Cheesecake

Lunch

68 Avocado Bars

70 Avocado Cheesecake

72 Berry Walnut Salad

74 Blueberry Grapefruit Walnut Salad with Blueberry Coconut Vinaigrette

76 Seafood Berry Peach Salad

78 Grapefruit Chef Salad

80 Chickpea Fruit Chopped Salad

82 Chickpea Pear Avocado Salad

84 Cinnamon Donuts

86 Cottage Cheese Peach Berry Salad

88 Creamy Grapefruit Tossed Salad

90 Eggplant Panini

92 Lemon Souffle

94 Mini Strawberry Vanilla Clouds

96 Pumpkin Avocado Bars

98 Pumpkin Banana Cheesecake Pudding

100 Loaded Roasted Pears

102 Spicy Egg Bowl

104 Toasted Coconut Limesicle

106 Tunamatoes Bites

Dinner

114 Asian Cabbage Stir Fry

116 Avocado Egg Salad Wrap

118 BBQ Chicken Wraps

120 Slow Cooker Chicken Enchilada Soup

122 Chili

124 Creamy Taco Chicken Bowl

126 Eggs Pizzaiola

128 Cabbage Taco Wraps with Creamy Avocado Dressing Ingredients:

130 Veggie Lasagna Bowl

132 Sneaky Chickpea Soup

134 Cheesy Zucchini Soup

136 Cheesy Cauliflower Broccoli Bake

Sauces, Seasonings, and Sides

140 Blueberry Coconut Vinaigrette

142 Lemon Dijon Vinaigrette

144 Red Wine Vinaigrette

146 Ranch Roasted Chickpeas

Food addiction is not like other addictions. Most addictions you can stop cold turkey, but you can't exactly do that with food. Most diets fail, are not realistic, or are not sustainable. "Run 20 miles, do 30 burpee's, then hike Mount Everest. You will be skinny in no time!" or "Eat our pre-made food… it tastes like cardboard and you will be starving most of the time." Or "Eat only baked fish and broccoli" or "Take these pills and drink this potion and BAM thin!" These yo-yo diets do not deal with the real problem and you can't live on pills or climb Mount Everest forever… so the weight comes back.

What if I told you there was a better way to lose weight, be healthy, and keep the weight off? You even get to eat a lot of delicious food without starving the whole time! If I can do it, a chunky kid who loved pizza, ice cream, and mac & cheese, you can do it! I will give you all the recipes (that's the hard part).

Sugar free, flour free, 3 weighed meals a day (no snacks in between). Deliciously FREE!

With Joy, Natalie

Breakfast

Breakfast = 1 protein, 1 fruit (6oz), and 1 grain.

Layer and layers of delicious!

7 Layer Banana Split

Ingredients:

1oz total: Shredded wheat, puffed kamut, uncooked oats (full grain)

2oz Plain Greek yogurt (1/2 protein)

1oz total: Sunflower kernels, cashews, walnuts, macadamia nuts, peanuts (1/2 protein)

6oz total: 1 Small banana, frozen blueberries, frozen strawberries (full fruit)

Pinch of each: Nutmeg, sea salt, cinnamon, vanilla extract.

1/2oz Peanut butter (1/4 protein)

Directions: Add frozen fruit and vanilla to a bowl and microwave 1min. Slice banana the long way. Layer banana, yogurt, fruit, nuts, grains, and seasonings. Drizzle peanut butter on top.

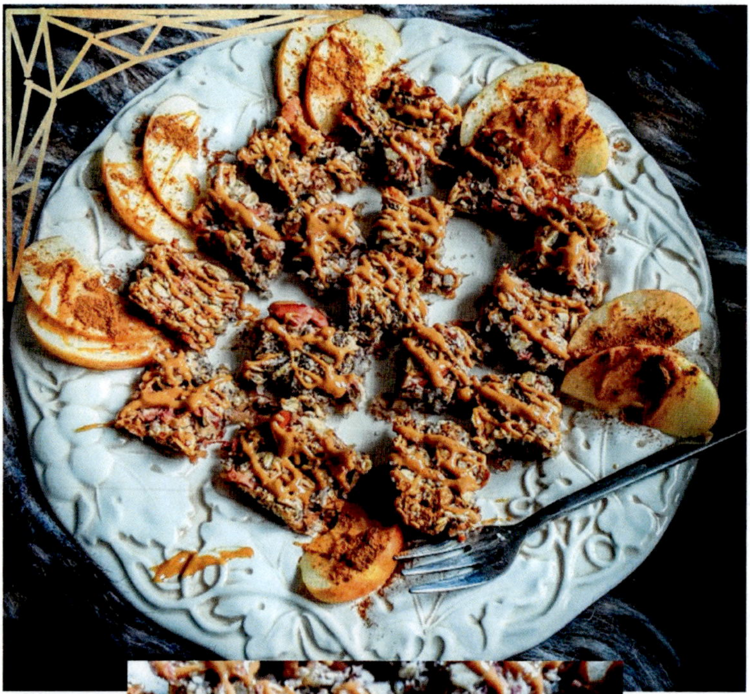
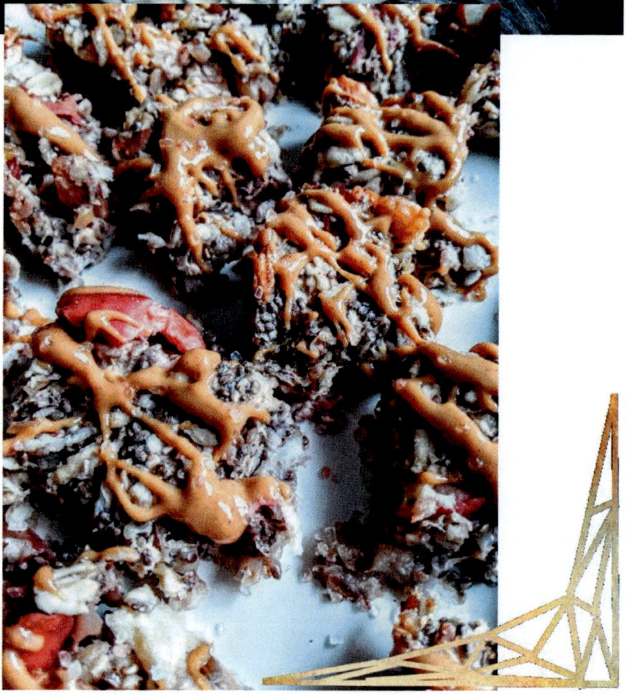

Applelicious Chia Bars

Ingredients:

1/2oz Chia seeds (1/4 protein)

6Tbsp Water

1oz Uncooked oats (full grain)

1oz total: Walnuts, pecans, peanuts, almonds (1/2 protein)

1/2oz Peanut butter (1/4 protein)

4oz Apple (2/3 fruit)

Sea salt

Directions: Preheat oven to 280. Mix water and chia seeds, let sit to thicken. Shred apple. Add nuts to a food processor and pulse until they are small pieces. Mix nuts, chia gel, oats, shredded apple, and salt. Press mixture into a lightly oiled baking dish. Bake 1hr 10min. Cut into bars. Set oven to 320 and bake bars again for 5min or until golden. Drizzle peanut butter on bars.

Side with 2oz fruit for a complete breakfast.

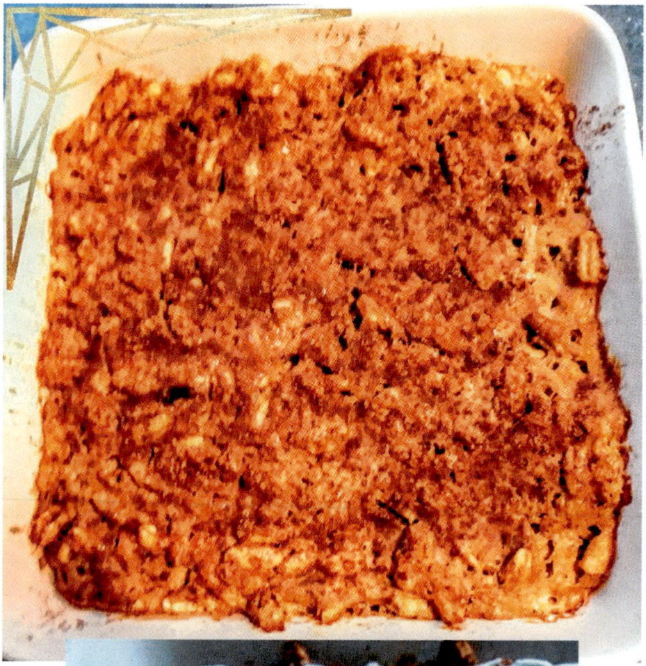

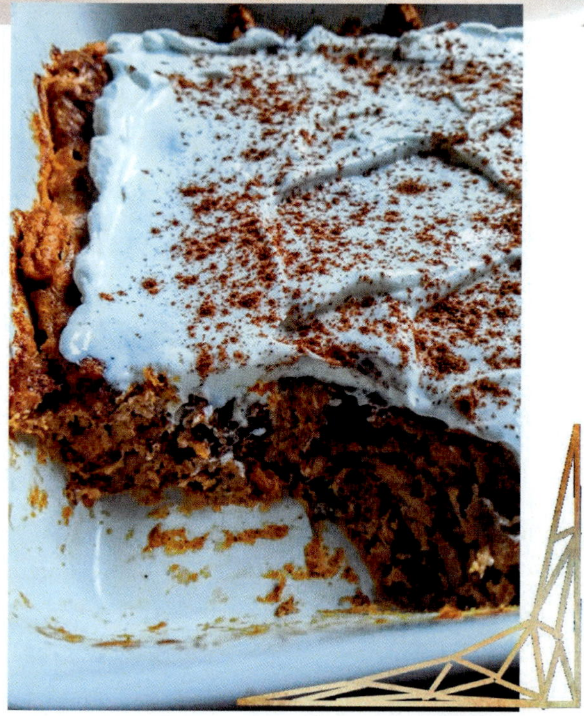

Baked Pumpkin Rice Crispy Bar

Ingredients:

3oz Pumpkin (1/2 fruit)

3oz Banana (1/2 fruit)

1oz Puffed kamut (full grain)

1 Egg (1/2 protein)

1/2oz Peanut butter (1/4 protein)

Pinch of each: Sea salt, almond extract, cinnamon, nutmeg, allspice

2oz Plain Greek yogurt (1/4 protein)

Directions: Preheat oven to 350. Mash banana. Add all ingredients except yogurt and mix. Pour mixture into a small oiled baking dish. Sprinkle with more seasonings and bake 20min. Top with Greek yogurt and a sprinkle of cinnamon.

Who knew that beans and rice make a delicious waffle!

Beans and Rice Waffle

Ingredients:

4oz Cooked rice (full grain)

3oz Black beans (1/2 protein)

1 Egg (1/2 protein)

3oz Banana (1/2 fruit)

Pinch of each: Sea salt, vanilla extract, nutmeg

1/2tsp Cinnamon

3oz Frozen blueberries (1/2 fruit)

Directions: Heat and lightly oil a waffle iron. Mash banana and black beans. Add remaining ingredients except blueberries and mix. Pour mixture into waffle iron and cook 10-15min. In a separate bowl add blueberries and microwave 2min. Top waffle with blueberries.

Blueberry Cobbler for breakfast? Yes please!

Blueberry Cobbler Oatmeal

Ingredients:

1oz Uncooked oats (full grain)

1oz Ricotta cheese (1/4 protein)

1/2oz Chia seeds (1/4 protein)

7oz Water

Pinch of each: Sea salt, vanilla extract, cinnamon

4oz Plain Greek yogurt (1/2 protein)

6oz total: Banana, frozen blueberries (full fruit)

Directions: Mix oats, ricotta, chia seeds, water, salt, vanilla, and blueberries. Microwave 2min. Chop banana. Stir banana into oatmeal. Top oatmeal with yogurt and cinnamon.

Layers of refreshing lemon, sweet blueberries, crunchy kamut, and banana cream!

Blueberry Lemon Parfait

Ingredients:

1oz Puffed kamut (full grain)

8oz Plain Greek yogurt (full protein)

2oz Lemon juice

2oz Banana (1/3 fruit)

4oz Frozen blueberries (2/3 fruit)

Cinnamon

Directions: Mash banana. Add 6oz Greek yogurt, 2oz lemon juice and mix. In a separate bowl, add ½ of puffed kamut to the bottom of your bowl. Layer in order ½ lemon yogurt mixture, 1/3 blueberries, remaining puffed kamut, 1/3 blueberries, remaining lemon yogurt mixture, 1/3 blueberries, plain Greek yogurt, and a sprinkle of cinnamon.

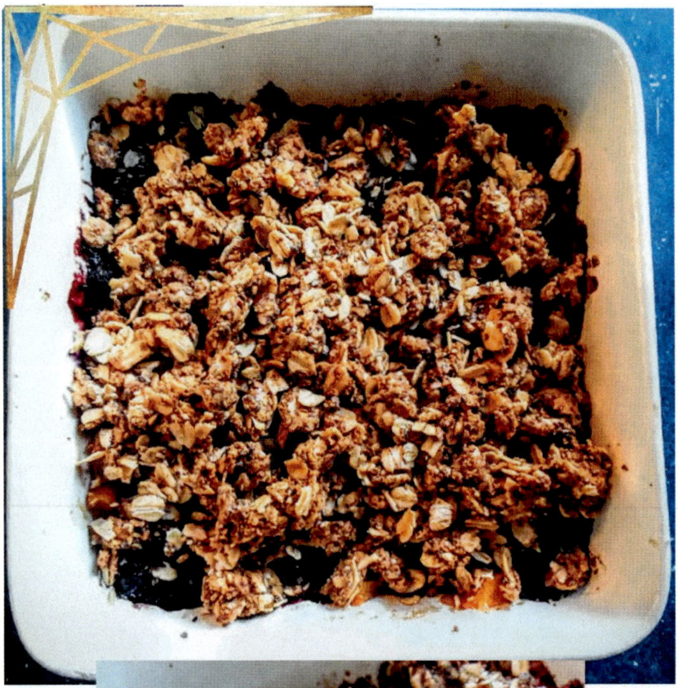

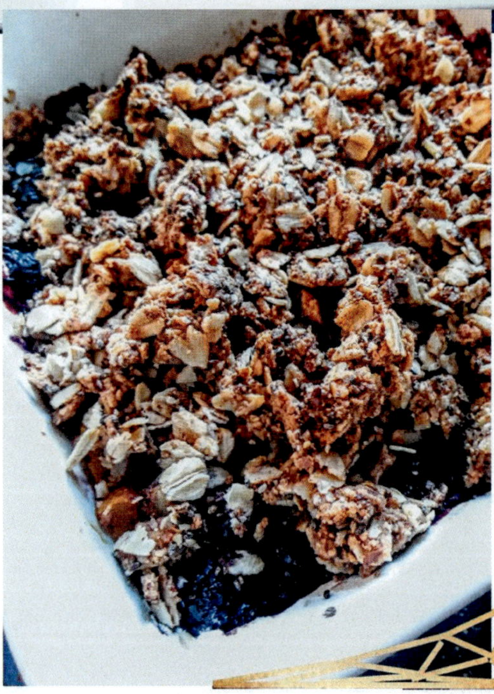

Blueberry Peach Crumble

Ingredients:

6oz total: Frozen blueberries, peaches (full fruit)

Pinch of each: Cinnamon, nutmeg, sea salt, arrowroot powder

1oz Uncooked oats (full grain)

1 1/2oz Peanut butter (3/4 protein)

1/2oz total: Ground flax seeds, hemp seeds (1/4 protein)

Directions: Preheat oven to 350. Place frozen blueberries, peaches and a pinch of arrowroot powder in an oven safe dish and lightly mix. In a separate bowl mix cinnamon, nutmeg, and salt. Spread the crumbly mixture on top of berries and bake for 30 mins.

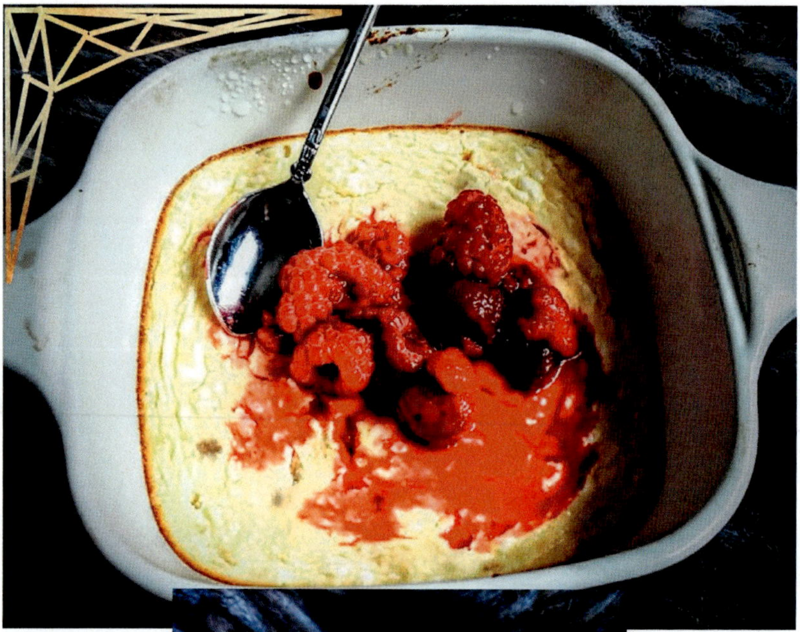

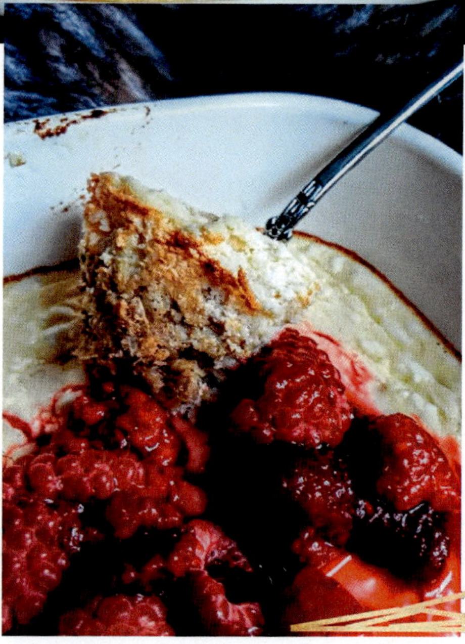

Breakfast Cheesecake with Oatmeal Crust

Ingredients:

2oz Plain Greek yogurt (1/4 protein)

1/2oz Cream cheese (1/4 protein)

1 Egg (1/2 protein)

5oz Banana (5/6 fruit)

Pinch of each: Sea salt, vanilla extract, cinnamon, nutmeg

1Tbsp Lemon juice

1oz Uncooked oats (full grain)

Directions: Preheat oven to 350. Mash 2oz banana. Add oats, cinnamon, nutmeg, sea salt to banana and mix. Lightly oil a small baking dish. Pour oat mixture into dish and cook 10min. In a separate bowl, mash remaining banana. Add remaining ingredients to banana and mix. Pour cheesecake mixture onto crust and bake 20min. Cake will have a slight jiggle. Refrigerate 4hr-overnight.

Top with 1oz fruit for a complete breakfast.

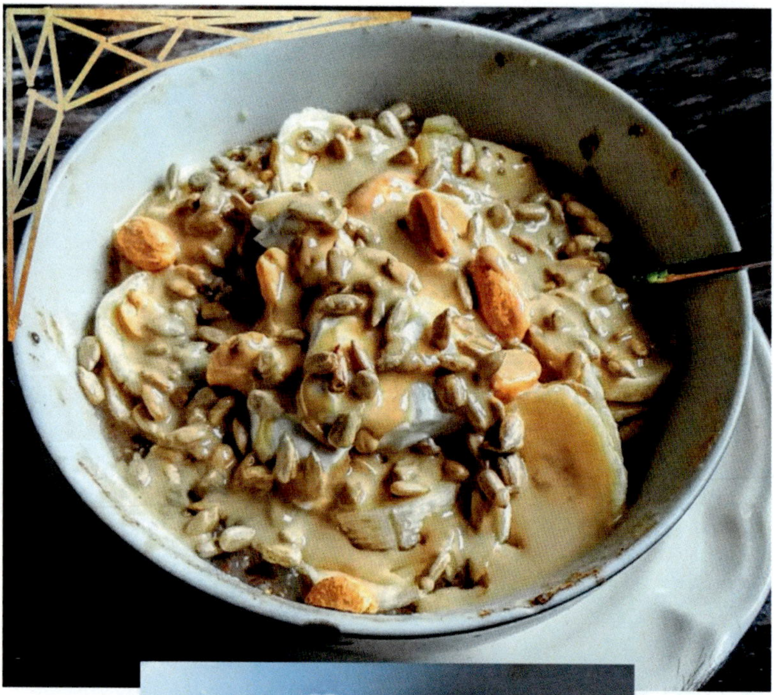

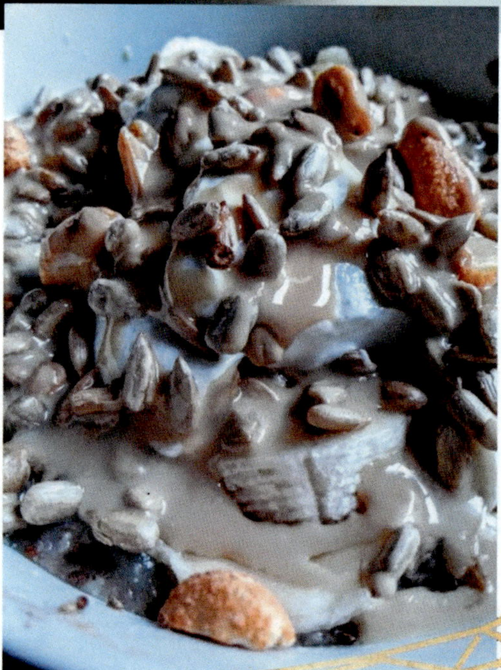

Dreamy Creamy Tahini Oatmeal

Ingredients:

6oz Banana (full fruit)

1/2oz Chia seeds (1/4 protein)

1/2oz total: Peanuts, roasted sunflower kernels (1/4 protein)

2oz Plain Greek yogurt (1/4 protein)

1/2oz Tahini (1/4 protein)

1oz Uncooked oats (full grain)

7oz Water

Pinch of each: Cinnamon, nutmeg, sea salt

Directions: Chop banana. Mix ½ banana, chia seeds, water, oats, and seasonings. Microwave 2min Top with remaining banana, Greek yogurt, nuts, and tahini.

Oh that crunch!!

Crunch Berry Parfait

Ingredients:

4oz Plain Greek yogurt (1/2 protein)

1/2oz Roasted chickpeas (1/4 protein)

1/2oz Peanut butter (1/4 protein)

6oz total: Frozen berries (full fruit)

1oz Shredded wheat (full grain)

Directions: Add yogurt to the bottom of your cup/bowl. In a separate bowl microwave berries 1min 30sec. Pour berries on top of yogurt. Top parfait with shredded wheat, roasted chickpeas, and drizzle with peanut butter.

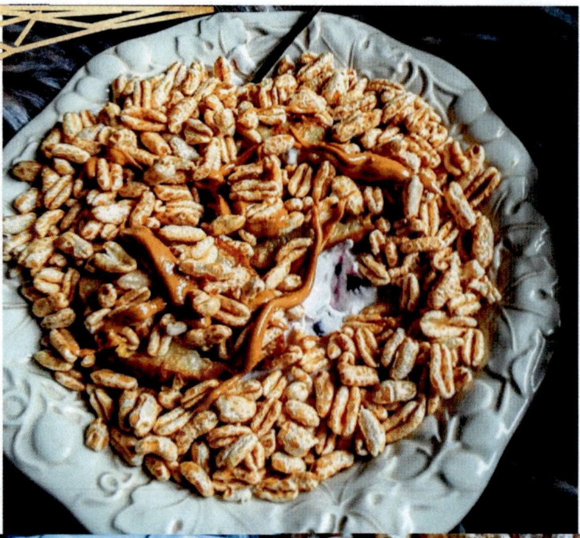

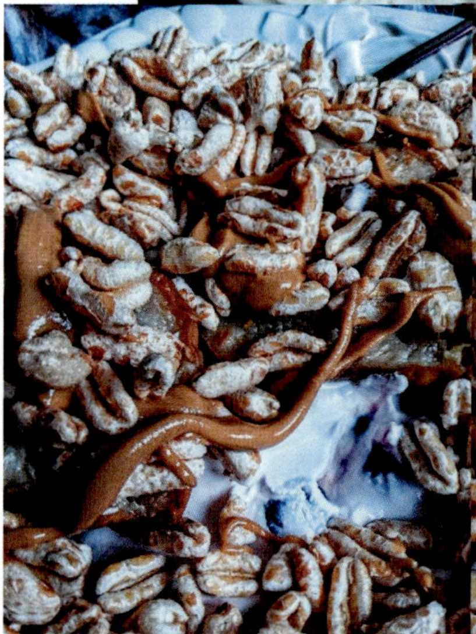

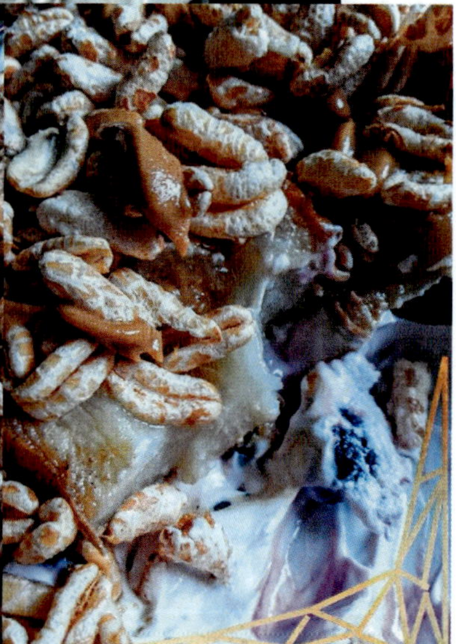

Blueberry Roasted Pear Crunch Bowl

Ingredients:

1oz Puffed kamut (full grain)

6oz total: Frozen blueberries, roasted pears (full fruit)

6oz Plain Greek yogurt (3/4 protein)

1/2oz Peanut butter (1/4 protein)

Directions: Preheat oven to 400. Lightly oil a baking sheet. Cut pears in half and remove core. Place pears skin side down on baking sheet. Spray pears with olive oil and roast 15-20min. Mix frozen blueberries and Greek yogurt. Top with roasted pears, puffed kamut and drizzle with peanut butter.

Lemony fresh.

Blueberry Lemon Chia Pudding

Ingredients:

3oz Banana (1/2 fruit)

3oz Blueberries (1/2 fruit)

Pinch of each: Lemon extract, sea salt

1\2oz Chia seeds (1\4 protein)

6oz Plain Greek yogurt (3/4 protein)

4oz Lemon juice

1/2oz Puffed kamut (1/2 grain)

½ Uncooked Oats (1/2 grain)

3oz Coffee or water

Directions: Mix 2oz lemon juice and chia seeds. Let sit to thicken. Add blueberries, salt, and lemon extract to a bowl and microwave 2min. Mash banana. Mix chia mixture, coffee, 2oz mashed banana, oats, 4oz yogurt and pour into a large cup or bowl. Pour blueberry mixture on top. In a separate bowl, mix 1oz mashed banana, 2oz lemon juice, 2oz Greek yogurt. Scoop lemon mixture on top and refrigerate overnight. In the morning top/side with 1oz puffed kamut.

Sweet frozen fruit with tart lime yogurt!

Fruity Limesicle Parfait

Ingredients:

6oz total: Banana, frozen blueberries, frozen cherries, frozen mango (full fruit)

1oz Lime juice

8oz Plain Greek yogurt (full protein)

1oz Puffed kamut (full grain)

Directions: Mash banana. Add remaining frozen fruit, lime juice, Greek yogurt, and mix. Top with puffed kamut.

38

Mango Toast

Ingredients:

1 Slice Ezekiel bread (full grain)

6oz Mango (full fruit)

1tsp Basil

2oz Ricotta cheese (1/2 protein)

Directions: Place bread in a toaster and toast. In a separate bowl mix mango and basil. Top toast with ricotta cheese and mango mixture. Broil 2-3min until cheese is slightly melted.

Side with ½ protein for a complete breakfast.

You'll go bananas for this peanut buttery breakfast

Monkey Chia Pudding

Ingredients:

6oz Banana (full fruit)

1oz Peanut butter (1/2 protein)

1/2oz Chia seeds (1/4 protein)

3oz Coffee or water

2oz Plain Greek yogurt (1/4 protein)

Pinch of Sea salt

1oz Puffed kamut (full grain)

Directions: Mash half of banana and slice the other half. Mix chia seeds, half of peanut butter, mashed banana, sliced banana, Greek yogurt, coffee, and salt. Top with remaining peanut butter. Refrigerate overnight. Top/side with puffed kamut.

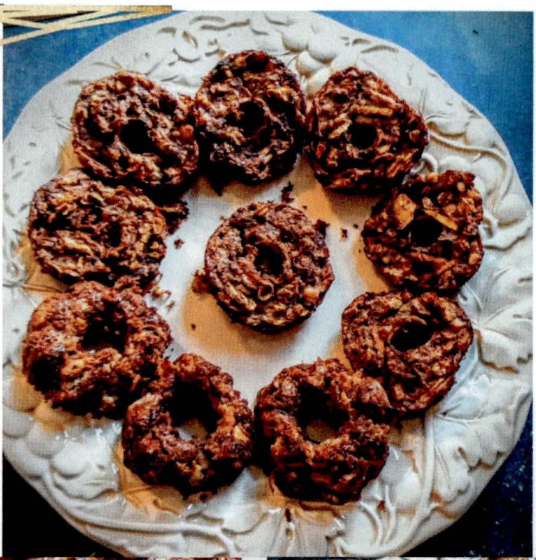
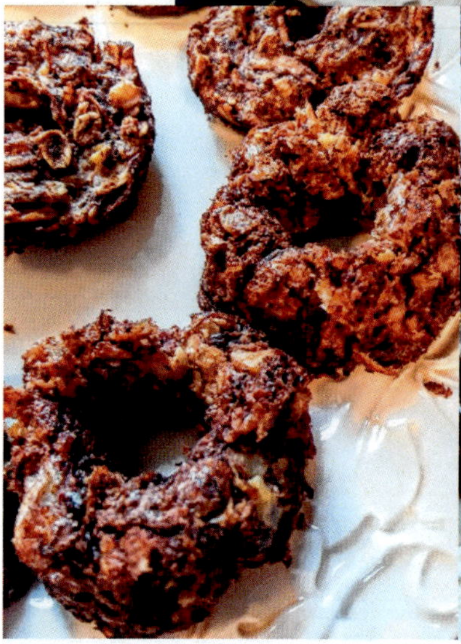
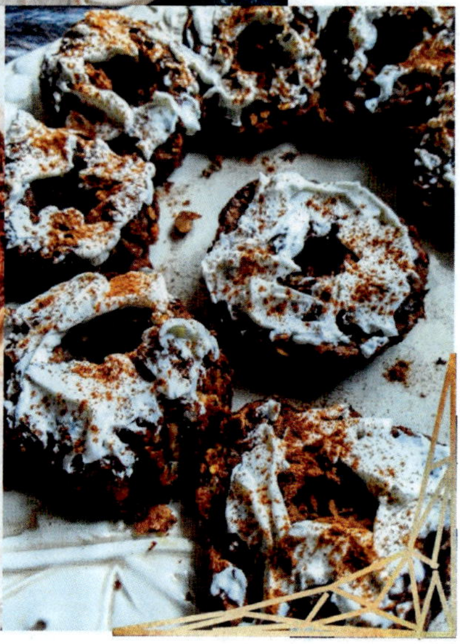

Morning Glory Donuts

Ingredients:
3oz Banana (1/2 fruit)
1/2oz Ground flax seeds (1/4 protein)
3Tbsp Warm water
Pinch of each: Sea salt, vanilla extract
3oz Chickpeas (1/2 protein)
1tsp Cinnamon + more for topping
1/2tsp of each: Ginger, baking soda
1oz Carrots (1/6 fruit)
2oz Apples (1/3 fruit)
1oz Uncooked oats (full grain)
1oz Milk (1/8 protein)
1oz Plain Greek yogurt (1/8 protein)

Directions: Preheat oven to 350. Mix flax seed and water, let sit to thicken. Blend chickpeas and vanilla. Mash banana. Mix milk, flax egg, banana, chickpea mixture and ginger. In a separate bowl mix salt, oats, baking soda, cinnamon. Mix everything together except Greek yogurt. Lightly oil a donut pan (or a muffin tin). Scoop batter onto pan and bake 22-25min. Top with Greek yogurt and cinnamon.

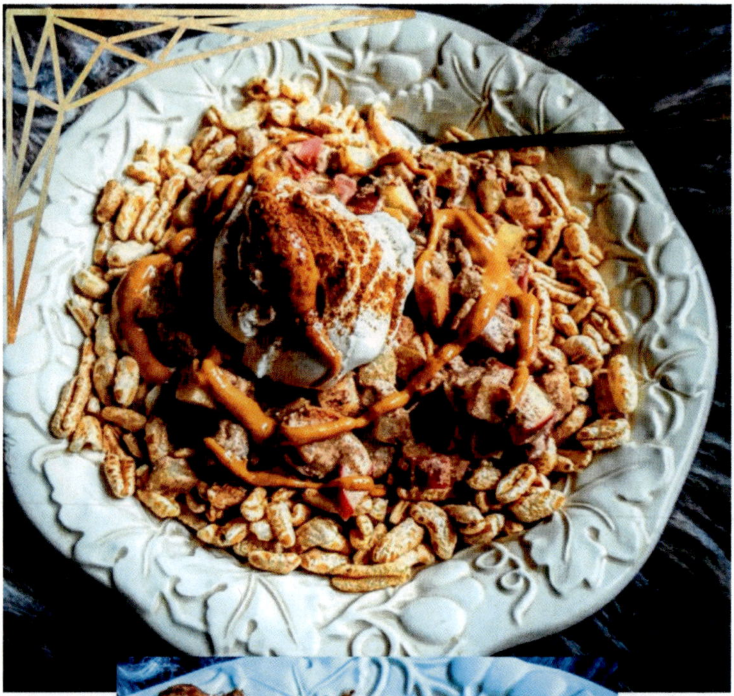

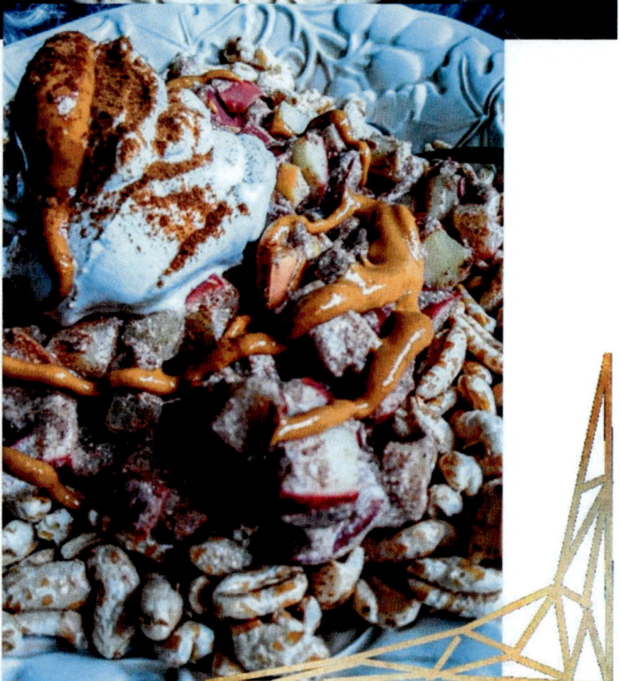

Peanut Butter Ricotta Apple Spice Bowl

Ingredients:

6oz Apple (full fruit)

1/2oz Lemon juice

2oz Ricotta cheese (1/2 protein)

1tsp Cinnamon

1/4tsp of each: Nutmeg, ginger

Pinch of each: Allspice, sea salt

1oz Puffed kamut (full grain)

2oz Plain Greek yogurt (1/4 protein)

1/2oz Peanut butter (1/4 protein)

Directions: Dice apple. Add diced apple, lemon juice, ricotta, and spices to a bowl and mix. Microwave 3min. Top hot apple mixture with puffed kamut, Greek yogurt and drizzle with peanut butter.

Pizza for breakfast? I think yes!

Pizza Rice Waffle

Ingredients:

4oz Cooked rice (full grain)

1 Egg (1/2 protein)

Pinch of each: Oregano, sea salt

2oz Spaghetti sauce (condiment)

1 1/2oz Ricotta cheese (3/8 protein)

1/2oz Turkey pepperoni (1/8 protein)

Directions: Heat and lightly oil a waffle iron. Mix rice, egg, and seasonings. Pour rice mixture into waffle iron and cook 7-8min or until steam stops coming out of the sides. In a separate bowl mix ricotta cheese and spaghetti sauce. Top waffle with ricotta mixture and pepperoni. Optional- Microwave pizza 1min to heat and melt cheese.

Mmm warm pancakes!

Pumpkin Apple Waffles

Ingredients:

Pinch of each: Cinnamon, pumpkin pie spice, sea salt, vanilla extract, baking powder

3oz Pumpkin (1/2 fruit)

3oz Apple (1/2 fruit)

1 Egg (1/2 protein)

1oz Uncooked oats (full grain)

1/2oz Almond butter or peanut butter (1/4 protein)

2oz Plain Greek yogurt (1/4 protein)

Directions: Heat and lightly oil a waffle iron. Shred apple. Mix all ingredients except almond butter and Greek yogurt. Pour mixture into waffle iron and cook 7-10min or until steam stops coming out of the sides. In a separate bowl mix almond butter and Greek yogurt. If mixture is too thick add a splash or two of water to thin. Top waffles with Fluff and a sprinkle of pumpkin spice.

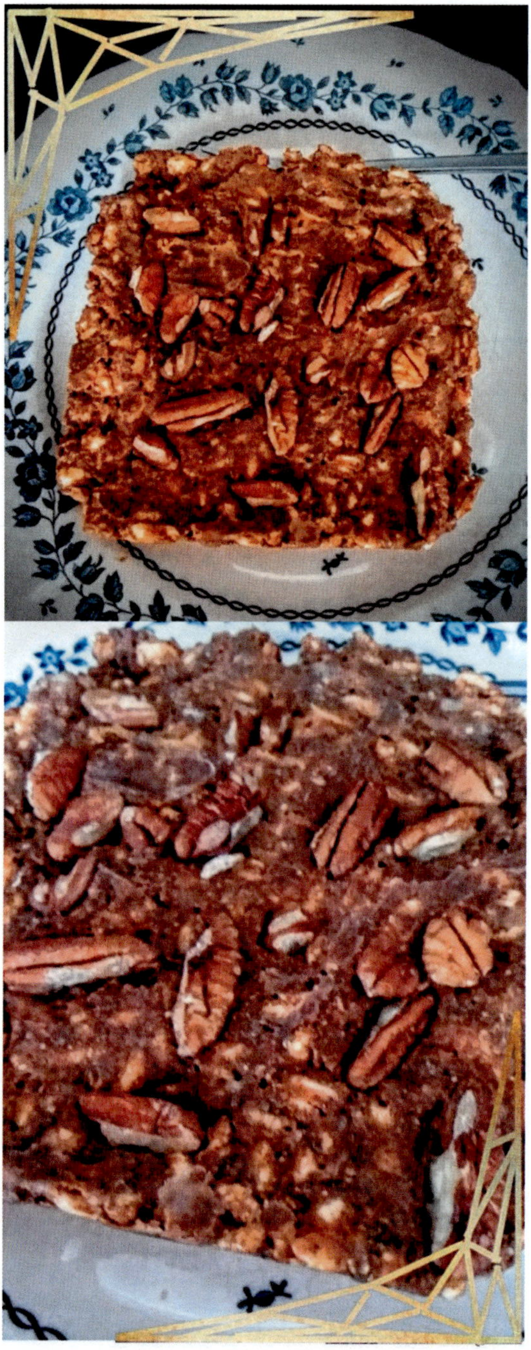

Pumpkin Rice Crispy Bar

Ingredients:

1/2oz total: Chia seeds, ground flax seeds (1/4 protein)

3oz Banana (1/2 fruit)

3oz Pumpkin (1/2 protein)

2tsp Pumpkin pie spice

1tsp Cinnamon

1oz Puffed kamut (full grain)

1oz Peanut butter (1/2 protein)

1/2oz Pecans (1/4 protein)

Directions: Mash banana. Add pumpkin, chia seeds, flax seeds, pumpkin spice, cinnamon, to banana and mix. In a separate bowl, mix peanut butter and puffed kamut. Press kamut mixture into a small baking dish and top with pumpkin mixture, Top with pecans and freeze 4-6hrs or overnight.

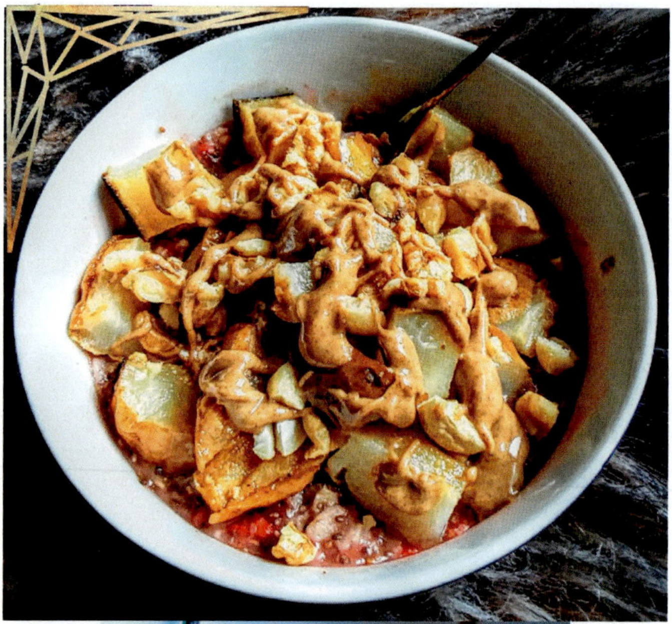

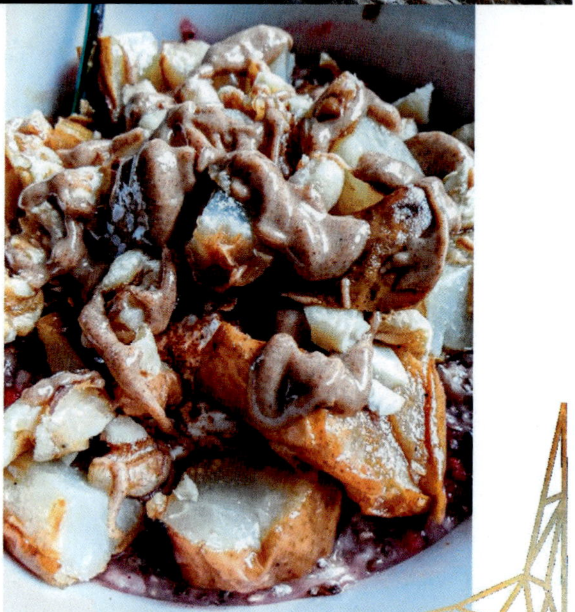

Roasted Pear Raspberry Oatmeal

Ingredients:

1oz Uncooked oats (full grain)

5oz Roasted pears* (5/6 fruit)

1oz Frozen raspberries (1/6 fruit)

2oz Plain Greek yogurt (1/4 protein)

1/2oz Chia seeds (1/4 protein)

Pinch of each: Nutmeg, cinnamon, sea salt

1/2oz total: Cashews, walnuts (1/4 protein)

1/2oz Almond butter or peanut butter (1/4 protein)

7oz Water

Directions: Mix oats, raspberries, water, chia seeds, sea salt and microwave 2min. Chop roasted pears. Top oatmeal with pears, yogurt, nuts, seasonings, and drizzle with almond butter.

(if almond butter is too thick, add a splash of hot water and stir until smooth. Repeat until desired consistency)

*Find Roasted Pear recipe on page 32

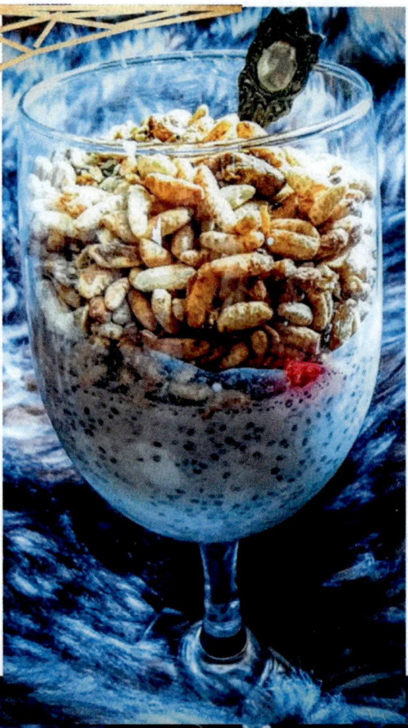

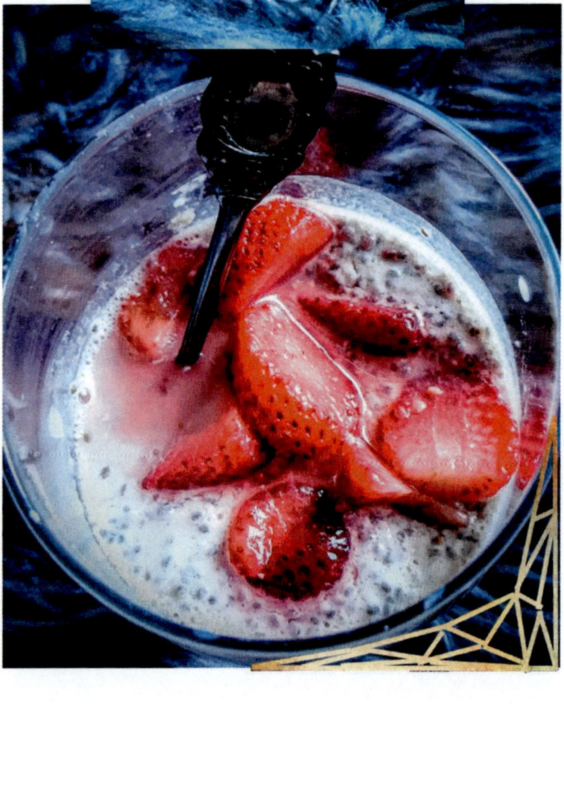

Strawberry heaven!

Strawberry Shortcake Chia Pudding

Ingredients:

6oz total: Strawberries, banana (full fruit)

1\2oz Chia seeds (1\4 protein)

3oz Brewed coffee or water

2oz Plain Greek yogurt (1\4 protein)

Pinch of each: Sea salt, vanilla extract

Directions: Mash banana. Add all ingredients to a large glass or bowl and mix. Refrigerate overnight.

Side with 1 grain and 1\2 protein (or top with peanut butter granola from volume 1)

Oh so toasty!

Toasted Sweet Potato and Almond Butter Bowl

Ingredients:

4oz Sweet potato (full grain)

2oz Plain Greek yogurt (1/4 protein)

1/2oz total: Walnuts, pecans, peanuts (1/4 protein)

6oz total: Apples, banana (full fruit)

1/2oz Almond butter or peanut butter (1/4 protein)

Pinch of each: Cinnamon, sea salt

Directions: Heat and lightly oil a skillet. Slice apples thin. Peel and dice sweet potato. Add sweet potato and apple to skillet and cook until tender. Top sweet potato with Greek yogurt, apples, nuts, and almond butter. If almond butter is too thick, add a splash of hot water and stir until completely combined, repeat until desired consistency. Sprinkle everything with cinnamon and sea salt.

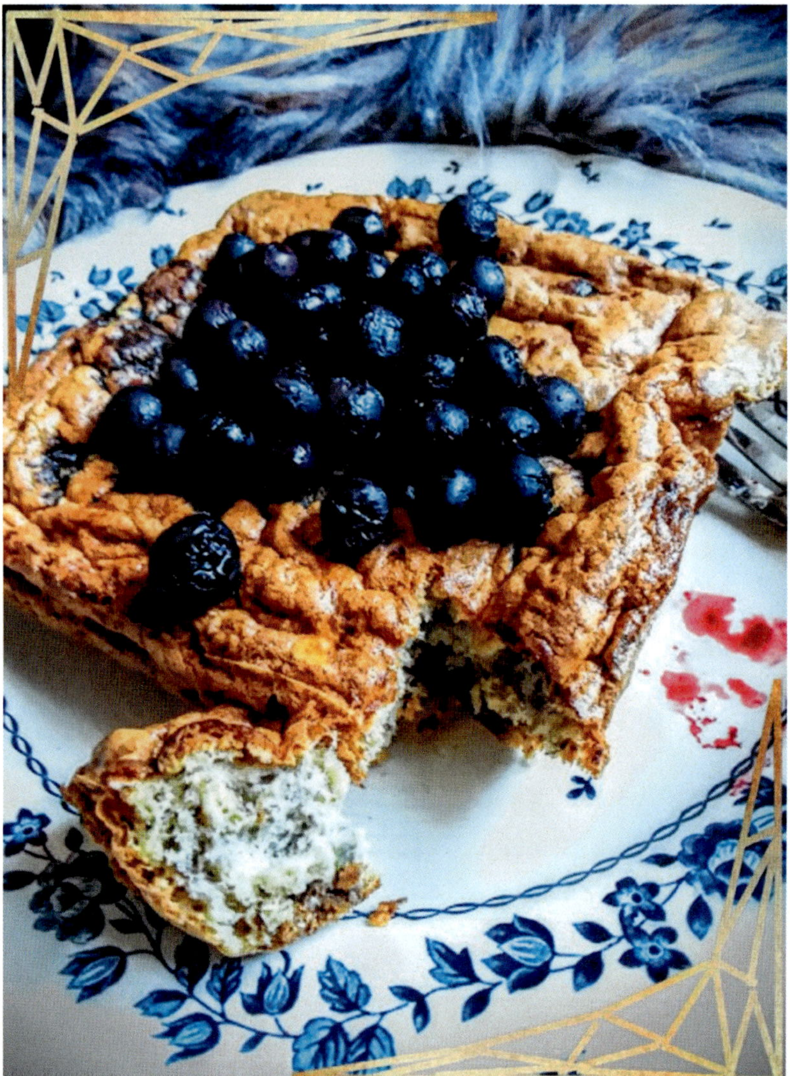

Vanilla Sponge Cake

Ingredients:

2 Eggs separated (full protein)

4oz Banana (2/3 fruit)

2tsp Vanilla extract

1oz Uncooked oats (full grain)

1/2tsp Baking powder

1/4tsp Baking soda

Pinch of sea salt

Directions: Preheat oven to 350. Line a medium baking dish with parchment paper. Whip egg yolks 7-10min until light and fluffy. Mash banana and stir into whipped egg yolks. Whip egg whites and vanilla until stiff peaks form. Gently fold all ingredients together 1/3 at a time making sure you do not deflate egg whites and yolks. Pour mixture into lined dish. Bake 45min until golden brown.

Top with 2oz fruit for a complete breakfast.

Lemon blueberry heaven!!

Blueberry Lemon Breakfast Cheesecake

Ingredients:

2oz Lemon juice

4oz Plain Greek yogurt (1/2 protein)

1 Egg (1/2 protein)

Pinch of each: Sea salt, vanilla extract, cinnamon, nutmeg

3oz Banana (1/2 fruit)

1oz Blueberries (1/6 fruit)

1oz Uncooked oats (full grain)

2oz Banana (1/3 fruit)

Directions: Preheat oven to 350. Mash 2oz banana. Add oats, cinnamon, nutmeg, sea salt and mix. Lightly oil a small baking dish. Pour oat mixture into dish and cook 10min. In a separate bowl, mash remaining banana. Add remaining ingredients and mix. Pour cheesecake mixture onto crust and bake 20min. Cake will have a slight jiggle. Refrigerate 4hr-overnight.

Lunch

Lunch = 1 protein, 1 fruit (6oz), 6oz vegetables, and 1 fat.

"Help! I'm being tempted by food!!"

Have you noticed that every time we are tempted with food it's when we are tired, when our meal didn't live up to the expectation we thought it would, when you can't eat one more sprig of broccoli? I have too. At those times, I have noticed there are a couple things that seem to pop up. One of them is, not being thankful.

There was a study done in 1995. In this study, 186 patients who were grateful and thankful reported having better sleep, less fatigue, less depression, more confidence in their ability to care for themselves, and lower levels of systemic inflammation.

Gratitude is good for our brains

For those of us who did not pay attention in biology class: the hypothalamus is the part of our brain that regulates a number of our bodily functions including our appetites, sleep, temperature, metabolism and growth. A 2009 National Institutes of Health (NIH) study showed that our hypothalamus is activated when we feel gratitude, or display acts of kindness.

Acts of kindness and feelings of gratitude flood our brains with a chemical called dopamine. When we are truly grateful for something (or someone) our brains reward us by giving us a natural high. Because this feeling is so good, we are motivated to feel it again and become more inclined to give thanks, and to do good for others also.

The same thing happens in our brain when we eat junk food. Our brain releases dopamine and gives us that happy feeling. However, if we focus our brain and life to be rewarded with thankfulness and doing good things, that will be our new release of dopamine! And I believe it lasts much longer than just eating junk food. My mother always reminds herself, (and me) when I'm craving those junk foods, "How long will the satisfaction of that one bite or piece of junk food last? 5 minutes? 3 minutes? Then you will be craving more and more." To me, that is not worth it!

Research on gratitude benefits shows that these neurological effects open the doors to many health benefits including:

1. Decreased Pain Levels

2. Better Sleep

3. Stress Relief

4. Reduced Anxiety and Depression

5. Increased Energy and Vitality

Gratitude can help reduce stress. Stress can lead to weight gain and stress eating. When a stressful situation or life event occurs, place your focus on what IS going well instead of what isn't. Doing this can help take attention away from the problem.

In a research study on gratitude in 1998, subjects were made to cultivate appreciation. Twenty-three percent showed a decrease in cortisol—the most prominent stress hormone. Even more impressive is that 80% of participants showed changes in heart rate variability; a direct result of reduced stress levels.

Cortisol can also slow or even stop weight loss in the body because chronic stress produces hormonal and immune factors that are contributors to being overweight. These biochemicals can also affect appetite and eating behaviors that can lead to emotional eating and even binge eating. That's not all! Gratitude benefits us by making us more resilient to trauma and stressful events. The GGSC underwent a study that proved that subjects who were grateful were faster in their recoveries after something traumatic, than those who weren't.

Gratitude research has repeatedly shown that thankful people have higher energy levels, are more relaxed, are happier, and are healthier. Naturally, these gratitude benefits have the potential to lengthen our lifespans.

John 10:10 (TPT) *But I have come to give you everything in abundance, more than you expect—life in its fullness until you overflow!*

(MSG) *I came so they can have real and eternal life, more and better life than they ever dreamed of.*

I have some homework for you. Every day, I want you to write down 5 things you are thankful for and see how your cravings will simply disappear! There is no room for cravings when you are full of thankfulness.

With joy and thankfulness,
Natalie

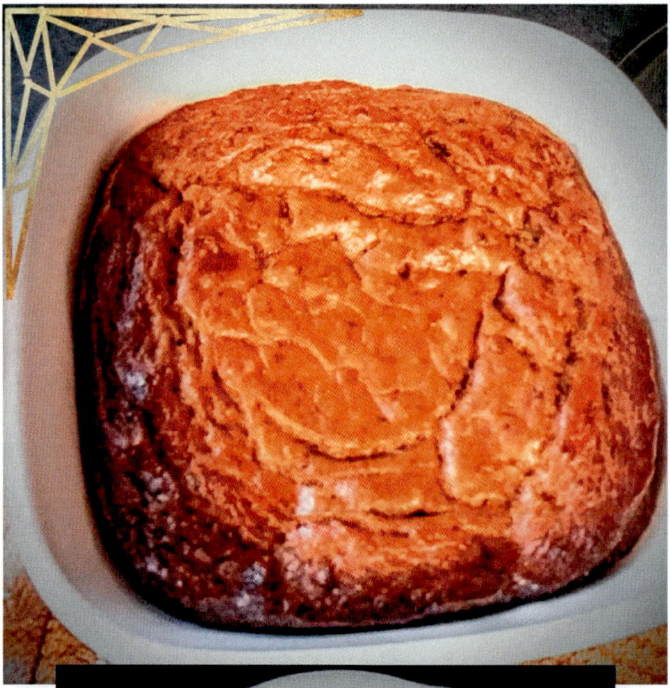

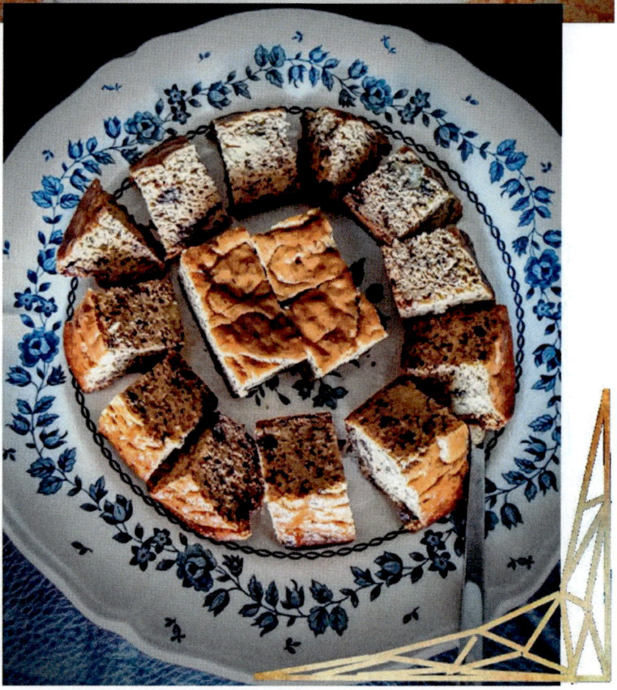

Avocado Bars

Ingredients:

3oz Banana (1/2 fruit)

1 Egg (1/2 protein)

3/4tsp Baking soda

Pinch of each: Sea salt, vanilla extract

1oz Peanut butter (1/2 protein)

1Tbsp Lemon juice.

2oz Avocado (full fat)

Directions: Preheat oven to 350. Mash banana and avocado. Add remaining ingredients except lemon juice and mix. Add lemon juice and mix. Pour mixture into a small lightly oiled baking dish and bake 20min or until a toothpick comes out clean.

Side with vegetables and 3oz fruit for a complete lunch

Super creamy!

Avocado Cheesecake

Ingredients:

3oz Banana (1/2 fruit)

2oz Avocado (full fat)

1 Egg (1/2 protein)

Pinch of each: Sea salt, vanilla extract

4oz Plain Greek yogurt (1/2 protein)

2Tbsp Lemon juice

3oz Frozen berries (1/2 fruit)

Directions: Preheat oven to 350. Mash banana and avocado. Add remaining ingredients and mix. Lightly oil a small baking dish. Pour mixture into baking dish and bake 20min. Refrigerate 4hrs-overnight. Add frozen berries to a bowl and microwave 1-2min. Pour berries on top of cheesecake

Side with vegetables for a complete lunch.

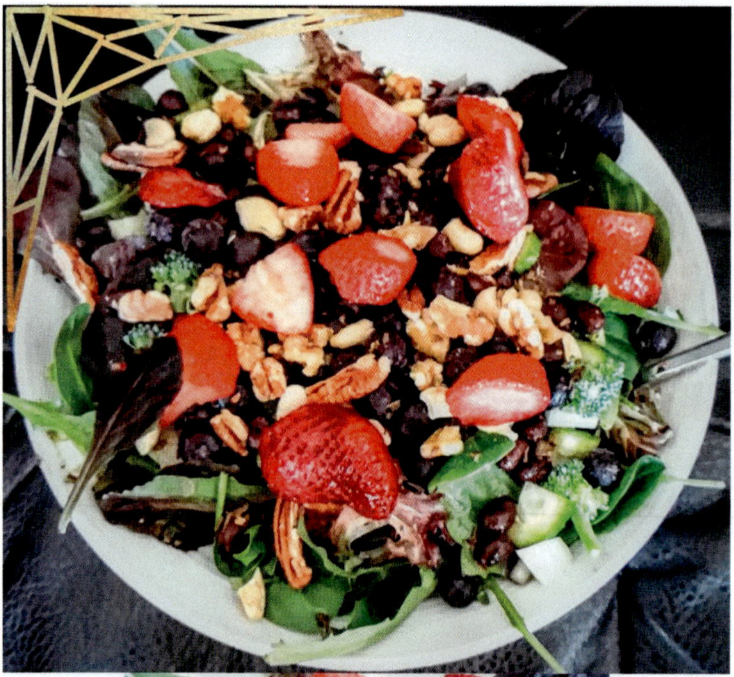

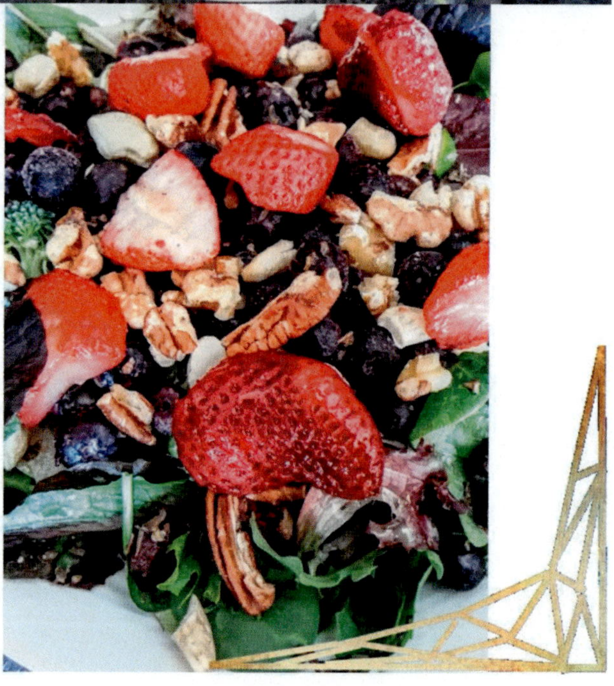

Berry Walnut Salad

Ingredients:

6oz total: Spring mix lettuce, onion, cucumber, broccoli (full vegetable)

6oz total: Frozen blueberries, frozen strawberries (full fruit)

3oz Black beans or 1oz Feta cheese (1/2 protein)

1 1/2oz Walnuts (1/2 protein + full fat)

*Red wine vinaigrette

Directions: Chop vegetables. Add spring mix to a large bowl and top with vegetables, frozen fruit, walnuts, and beans. Drizzle with vinaigrette.

*Find dressing in "Sauces, Seasonings, and Side's"

Colorful and delicious!!

Blueberry Grapefruit Walnut Salad with Blueberry Coconut Vinaigrette

Ingredients:

5oz total: Grapefruit, frozen blueberries (5/6 fruit)

6oz total: Spring mix lettuce, cucumber, green onion (full vegetable)

1oz Cottage cheese (1/4 protein)

1/2oz Walnuts (1/4 protein)

**Blueberry coconut vinaigrette (full fat + 1oz fruit)

1oz *Ranch roasted chickpeas (1/2 protein)

Directions: Dice/chop vegetables and grapefruit. Add vegetables to a large bowl. Top with fruit, cottage cheese, walnuts, and dressing.

*Find Ranch Roasted Chickpeas in "Sauces, Seasonings, and Sides"

**Find dressing in "Sauces, Seasonings, and Side's"

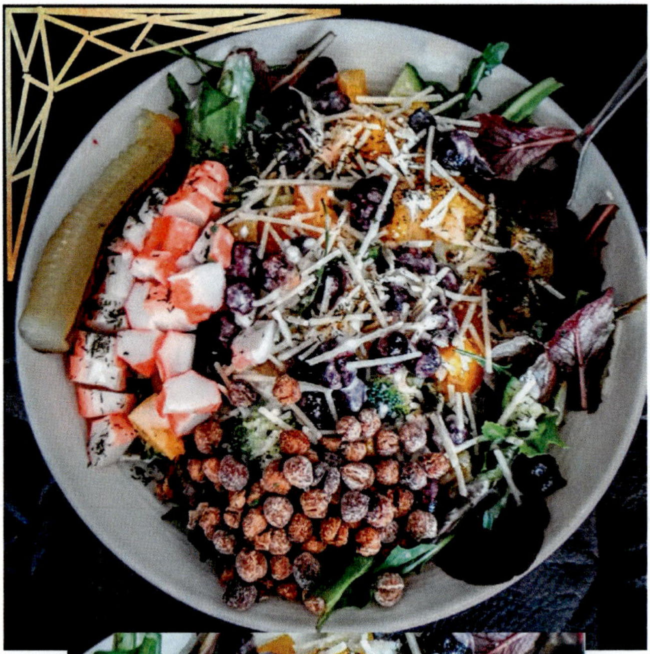

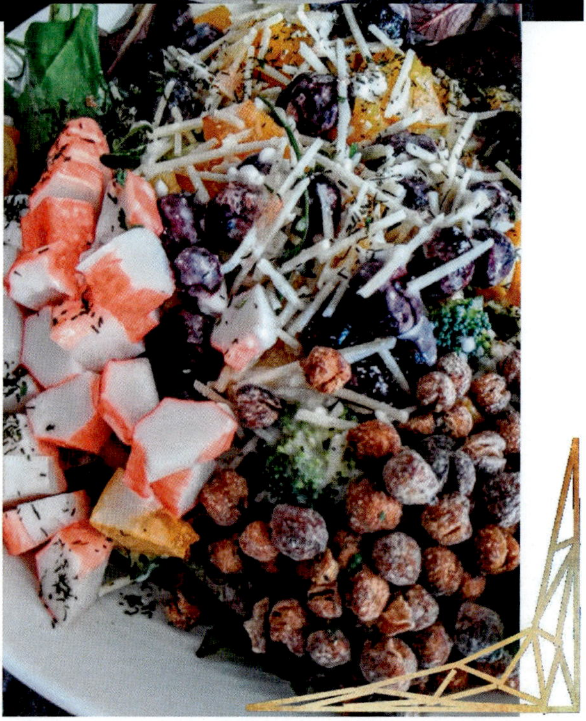

Seafood Berry Peach Salad

Ingredients:

6oz total: Peaches, frozen blueberries (full fruit)

6oz total: Spring mix lettuce, cucumber, green onion, broccoli (full vegetable)

2oz Crab meat (1/2 protein)

1oz *Roasted chickpeas (1/2 protein)

1/2oz Parmesan cheese (1/2 fat)

1oz Full fat canned coconut milk (1/2 fat)

1/2oz White wine vinegar

Directions: Chop/dice vegetables, peaches, and crab meat. Add vegetables to a large bowl. In a separate bowl mix coconut milk and white wine vinegar. Top salad with fruit, crab, chickpeas, cheese, and coconut vinegar dressing.

*Make sure to check your crabmeat ingredients for added sugar. *Find Ranch Roasted Chickpeas in "Sauces, Seasonings, and Sides"*

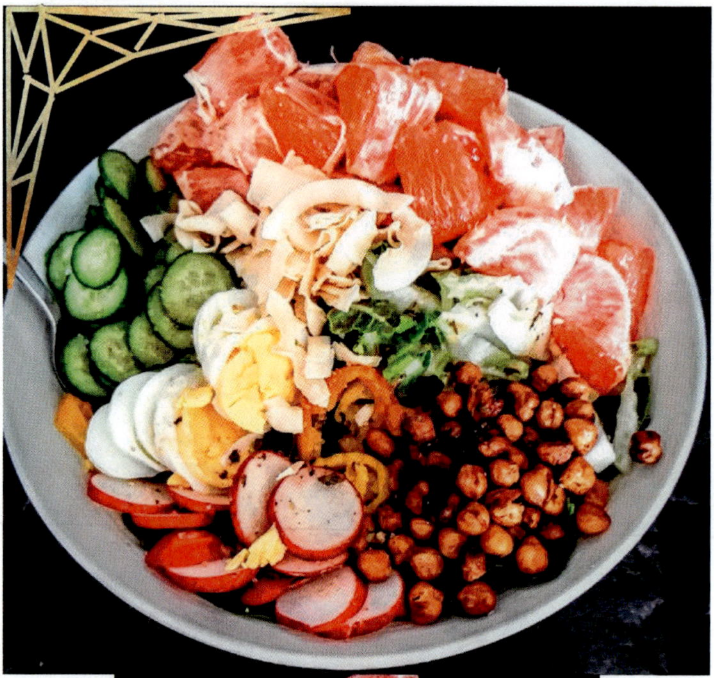

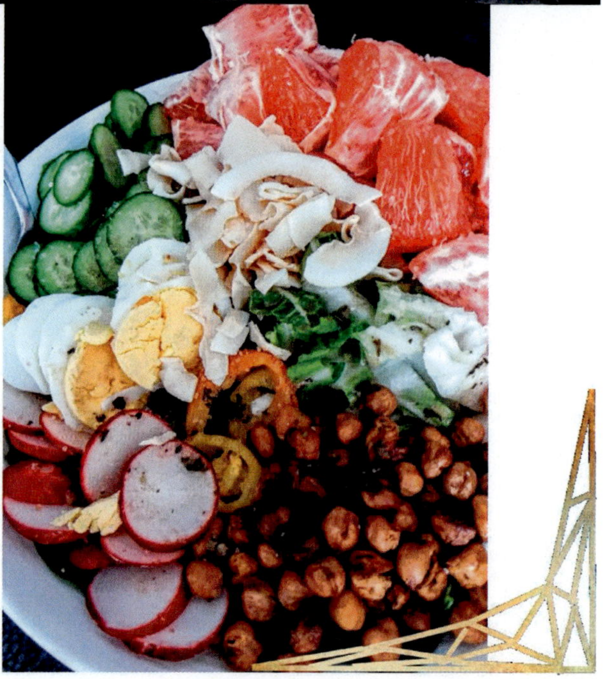

Grapefruit Chef Salad

Ingredients:

6oz total: Radish, cucumber, Napa cabbage, spring mix lettuce (full vegetable)

2oz Pickled banana peppers (condiment 2oz free)

1 Hardboiled egg (1/2 protein)

*Lemon Dijon Vinaigrette

1 Grapefruit (full fruit)

1/2oz Toasted coconut flakes (full fat)

1oz *Roasted chickpeas (1/2 protein)

Directions: Chop/dice vegetables, grapefruit, and hardboiled egg. Add vegetables to a large bowl. Top salad with remaining ingredients.

*Find Lemon Dijon Vinaigrette in "Sauces, Seasonings, and Side's

**Find Ranch Roasted Chickpeas in "Sauces, Seasonings, and Sides"

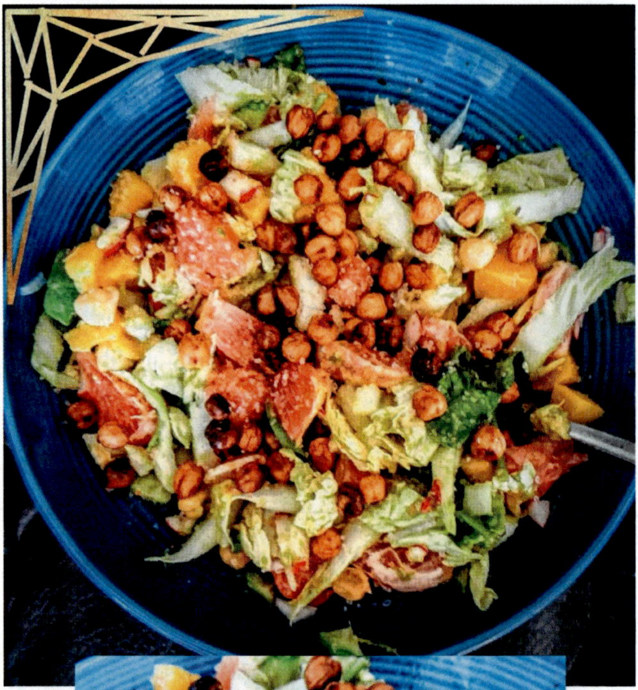

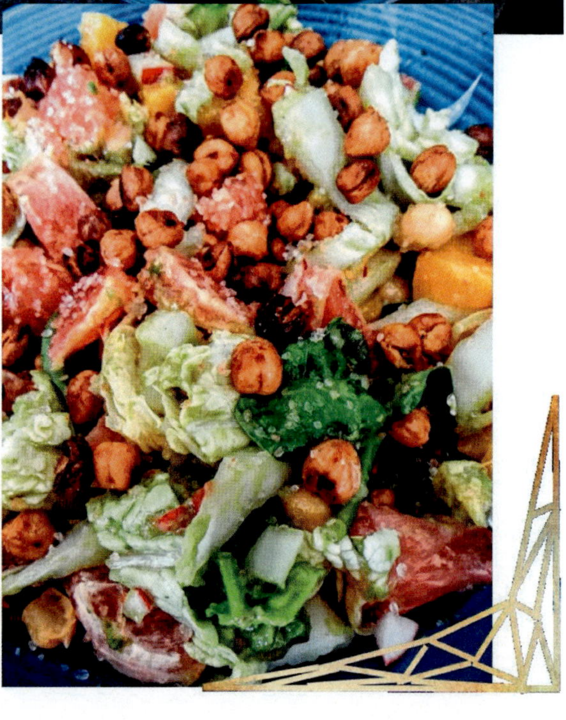

Chickpea Fruit Chopped Salad

Ingredients:

6oz total: Peach and mango (full fruit)

6oz total: Radish, Napa cabbage, cucumber, onion (full vegetable)

2oz Avocado (full fat)

3oz Canned chickpeas (1/2 protein)

1oz *Roasted chickpeas (1/2 protein)

**Red wine vinaigrette

Directions: Mash avocado. Chop vegetables and peach. Add all ingredients to a large bowl and mix. Drizzle with vinaigrette.

*Find Ranch Roasted Chickpeas in "Sauces, Seasonings, and Sides"

**Find dressing in "Sauces, Seasonings, and Side's"

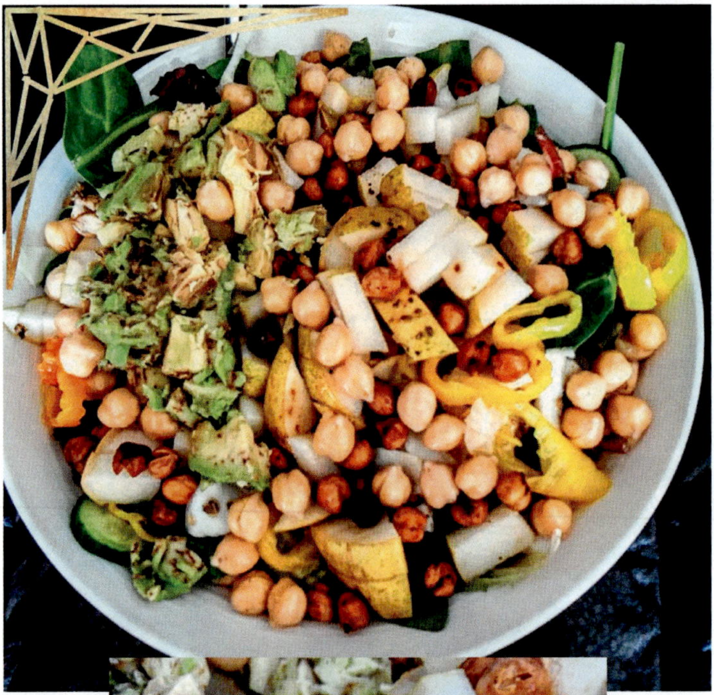

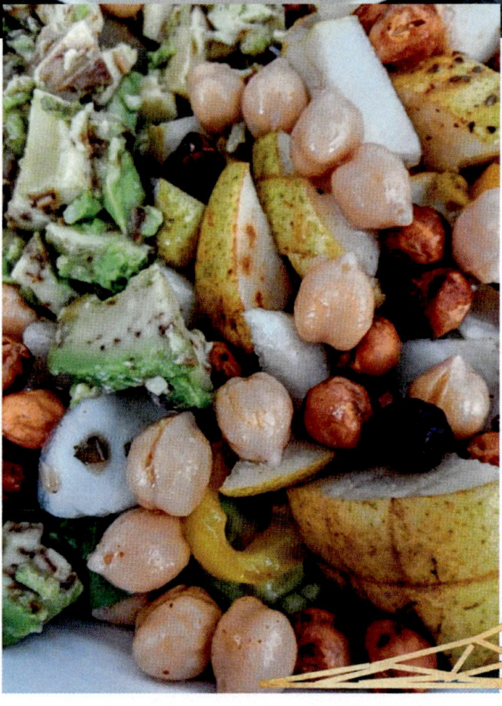

Chickpea Pear Avocado Salad

Ingredients:

6oz total: Spring mix lettuce, cucumber, cabbage, onion (full vegetable)

3oz Canned chickpeas (1/2 protein)

1oz *Roasted chickpeas (1/2 protein)

6oz Pears (full fruit)

2oz Avocado (full fat)

2oz Pickled banana peppers (condiment 2oz free)

**Red wine vinaigrette

Directions: Chop/dice vegetables, pears, and avocado. Add vegetables to a large bowl. Top salad with remaining ingredients and toss.

*Find Ranch Roasted Chickpeas in "Sauces, Seasonings, and Sides"

**Find dressing in "Sauces, Seasonings, and Side's"

Donuts for lunch!

Cinnamon Donuts

Ingredients:

1/2oz Ground flax seed (1/4 protein)

1/2oz Peanut butter (1/4 protein)

2oz Banana (1/3 fruit)

1 Egg (1/2 protein)

1Tbsp Butter (full fat)

1/2tsp Baking powder

1Tbsp Cinnamon + more for topping

1/2tsp Ginger

Sea salt

Directions: Preheat oven to 350. Mix all Ingredients. Lightly oil a donut pan (muffin pan or a baking sheet works in making these as cookies or muffins also.) sprinkle each donut with more cinnamon and sea salt. Bake 15min.

Side with 4oz fruit and 6oz vegetables for a complete lunch.

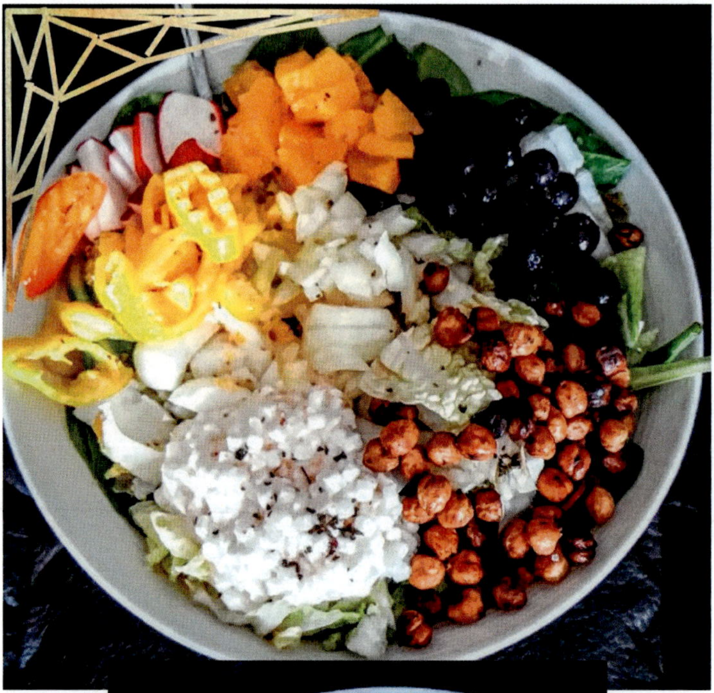

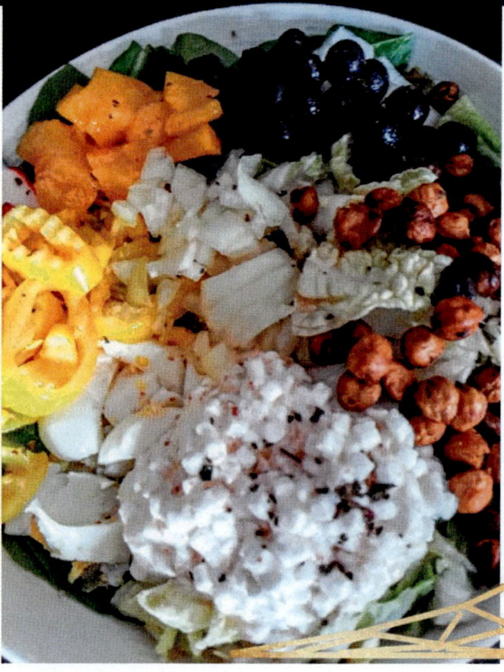

Cottage Cheese Peach Berry Salad

Ingredients:

6oz total: Radish, spring mix lettuce, onion, Napa cabbage (full vegetable)

2oz Cottage cheese (full fat)

6oz total: Peach, frozen blueberries (full fruit)

1oz *Roasted chickpeas (1/2 protein)

1 Hardboiled egg (1/2 protein)

2oz Pickles peppers (condiment)

**Red wine vinaigrette

Directions: Chop vegetables, egg, and peach. Add spring mix to a large bowl and top with fruit, cottage cheese, toasted chickpeas, egg, and peppers. Drizzle with vinaigrette.

*Find Red Wine Vinaigrette in "Sauces Seasonings and Side's" *Find Ranch Roasted Chickpeas in "Sauces, Seasonings, and Sides"

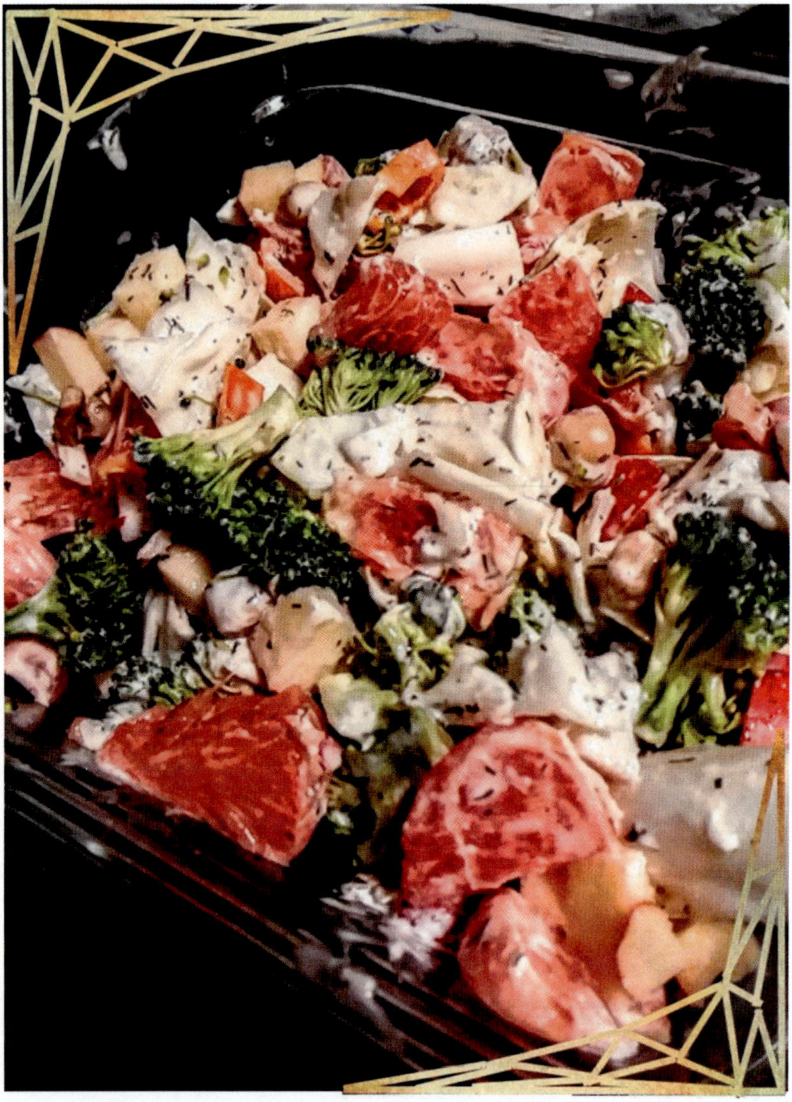

Creamy Grapefruit Tossed Salad

Ingredients:

6oz total: Cabbage, broccoli, radish, onion (full vegetable)

6oz total: Apple, grapefruit (full fruit)

2oz Plain Greek yogurt (1/4 protein)

3oz Chickpeas (1/2 protein)

1oz Walnuts (1/4 protein + full fat)

1/2oz *Red wine vinaigrette

1/2oz Lemon juice

1/4tsp Dill

1/8tsp Garlic salt

Directions: Chop/dice vegetables and fruit. Add all ingredients to a large bowl and mix.

*Find dressing in "Sauces, Seasonings, and Side's"

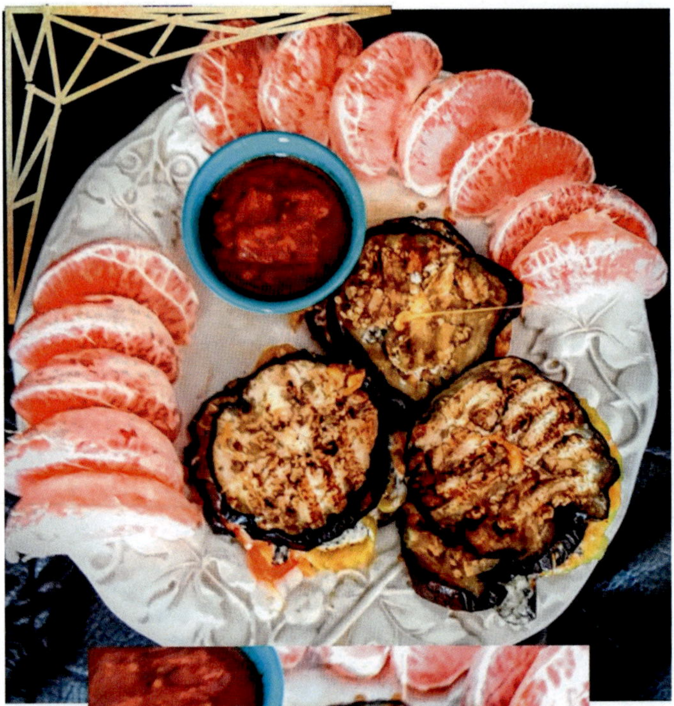
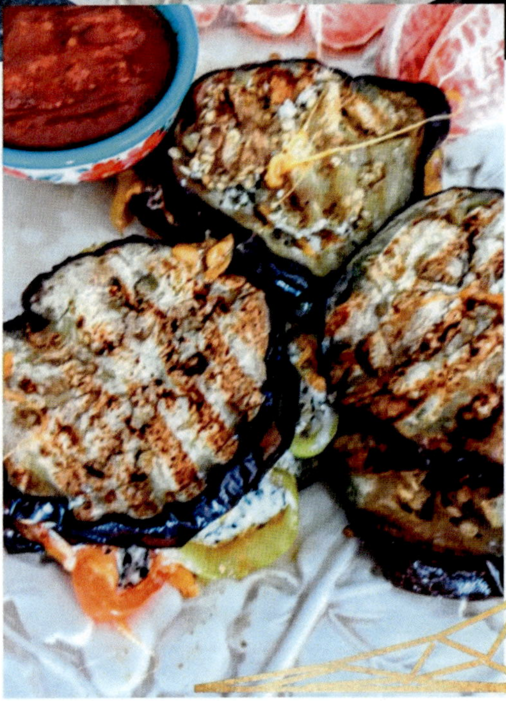

Eggplant Panini

Ingredients:

6oz Eggplant (full vegetable)

2oz Cheese (full protein)

2oz Ricotta cheese (full fat)

2oz Spaghetti sauce (condiment free up to 2oz)

Pinch of each: Garlic salt, onion powder, rosemary, parsley, oregano, basil

2oz Pickles banana peppers (condiment free)

Directions: Lightly oil a panini grill (or use a skillet). Slice eggplant and place on grill. Sprinkle with garlic salt and grill 2-3min. In a separate bowl mix ricotta and spices. Weigh 6oz grilled eggplant. Top with cheese, peppers, and ricotta mixture. Top with another slice of grilled eggplant and grill again 1-2min until cheese is melted.

Side with 6oz fruit for a complete lunch

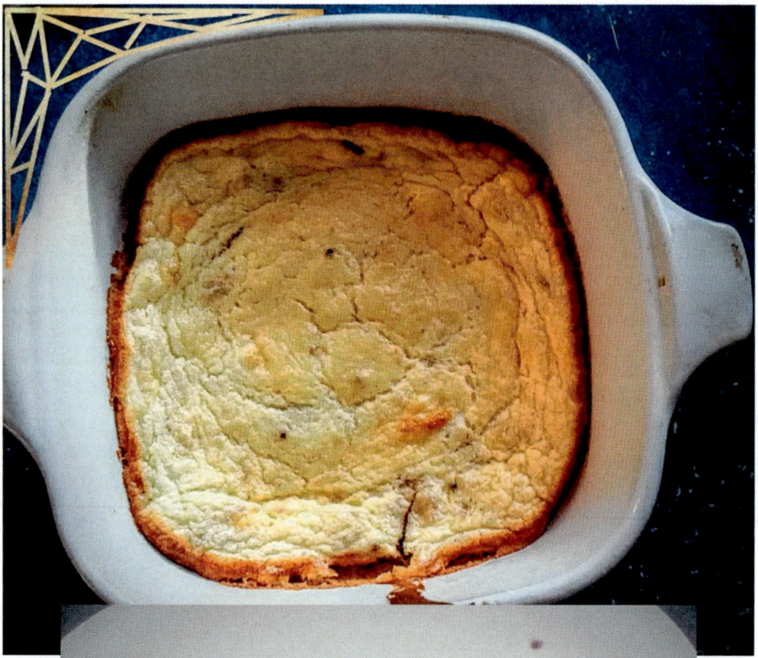

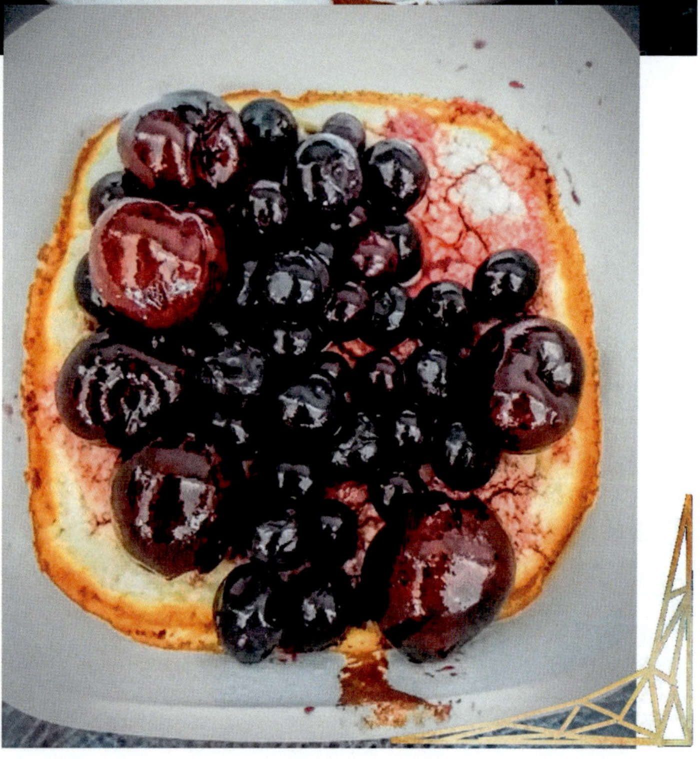

Lemon Souffle

Ingredients:

2oz Ricotta (1/2 protein)

1 Egg (separated) (1/2 protein)

2oz Banana (1/3 fruit)

1tsp Lemon zest

1Tbsp Lemon juice

1tsp Vanilla extract

Directions: Preheat oven to 375. Whip egg white until stiff peaks form. In a separate bowl, mash banana. Add egg yolk, ricotta cheese to mashed banana and mix. Also add lemon juice, zest, vanilla and mix well. Fold egg whites into mixture half at a time, stirring gently. Grease a small baking dish (or ramekin) and pour in batter. Bake 20min until the top is set but slightly jiggly.

Side with 4oz fruit, 1 fat, and 6oz vegetables for a complete lunch.

Donuts for lunch, I think YES!!

Mini Strawberry Vanilla Clouds

Ingredients:

1 Egg (separated) (1/2 protein)

1oz Cream cheese (full fat)

Pinch Cream of tartar

4tsp Vanilla extract

4oz Banana (2/3 fruit)

2oz Plain Greek yogurt (1/4 protein)

2oz Frozen strawberries (1/3 fruit)

Directions: Preheat oven to 300. Beat egg yolk, cream cheese, and 2tsp vanilla until smooth. Mash 2oz banana and stir into yolk mixture. In a separate bowl, whip egg white and cream of tartar until stiff peaks form. Gently fold both mixtures together making sure not to deflate egg whites. Scoop 2Tbsp of mixture into each lightly oiled donut mold. Bake 30-35min or until golden brown. In a separate bowl microwave frozen strawberry and remaining vanilla 2min. Add Greek yogurt and remaining banana to strawberries and lightly mash. Spread strawberry mixture onto cooled clouds.

Side with ¼ protein and 6oz vegetables for a complete lunch

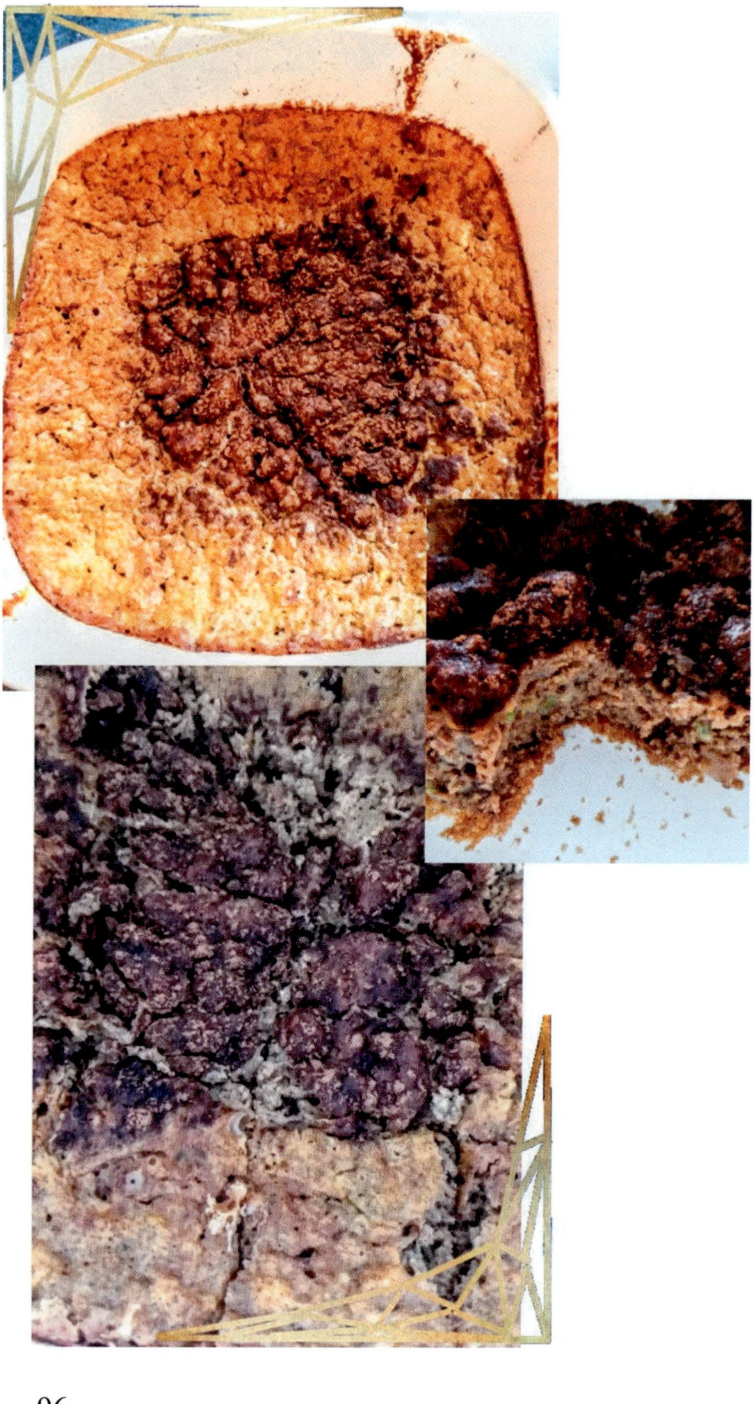

Pumpkin Avocado Bars

Ingredients:

3oz Banana (1/2 fruit)

3oz Pumpkin (1/2 vegetable)

1 Egg (1/2 protein)

Pinch of each: Sea salt, vanilla extract

1/2tsp Pumpkin pie spice

1tsp Cinnamon + more for topping

4oz Plain Greek yogurt (1/2 protein)

2Tbsp Lemon juice

1/4tsp Baking soda

2oz Avocado (full fat)

Directions: Preheat oven to 350. Mash banana, baking soda, and avocado. Add remaining ingredients and mix. Lightly oil a small baking dish and pour in mixture. Sprinkle with cinnamon. Bake 20min or until a toothpick comes out clean.

Side with 3oz fruit and 3oz vegetable for a complete lunch

Creamy and oh so delicious!

Pumpkin Banana Cheesecake Pudding

Ingredients:

3oz Pumpkin (1/2 vegetable)

3oz Banana (1/2 fruit)

1oz Whipped cream cheese (full fat)

1/2tsp of each: Cinnamon, pumpkin pie spice

Directions: Mash banana. Add all ingredients and mix.

Side with protein, 3oz fruit and 3oz vegetables for a complete lunch.

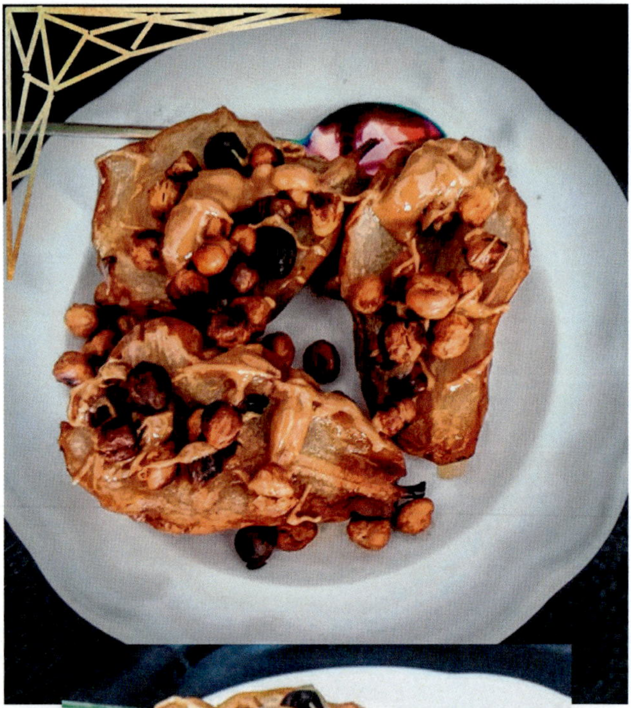
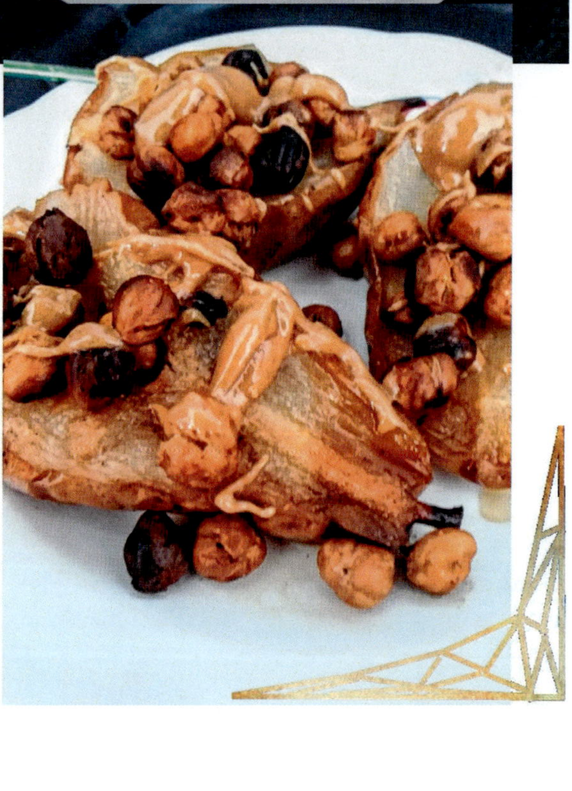

Loaded Roasted Pears

Ingredients:

6oz *Roasted pears (full fruit)

1oz Peanut butter (1/2 protein)

1oz **Roasted chickpeas (1/2 protein)

Directions: Top roasted pears with roasted chickpeas. Drizzle with peanut butter.

Side with vegetables, and a fat for a complete lunch

*Find roasted pears on page 32

**Find Ranch Roasted Chickpeas in "Sauces, Seasonings, and Sides"

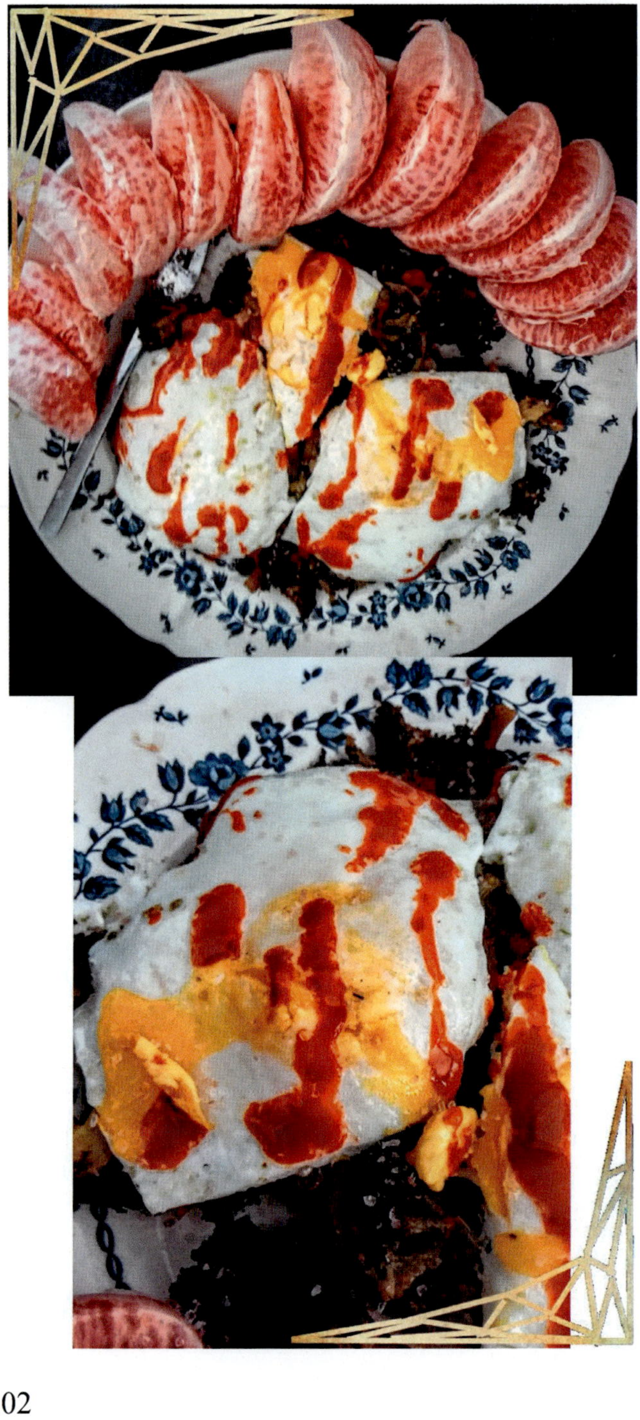

Spicy Egg Bowl

Ingredients:

1 Grapefruit (full fruit)

2 Egg (full protein)

Pinch of each: Sea salt, pepper

6oz total: Broccoli, spinach, colored peppers, onion (full vegetable)

Hot sauce

Directions: Heat and lightly oil a skillet. Chop/dice vegetables. Add vegetables (except spinach) to skillet and sauté. Once vegetables are tender add spinach and cook until wilted. Remove vegetables from skillet and lightly oil again. Cook eggs. Top vegetables with eggs, salt, pepper, and drizzle with hot sauce. Side with grapefruit.

Side with a fat for a complete lunch.

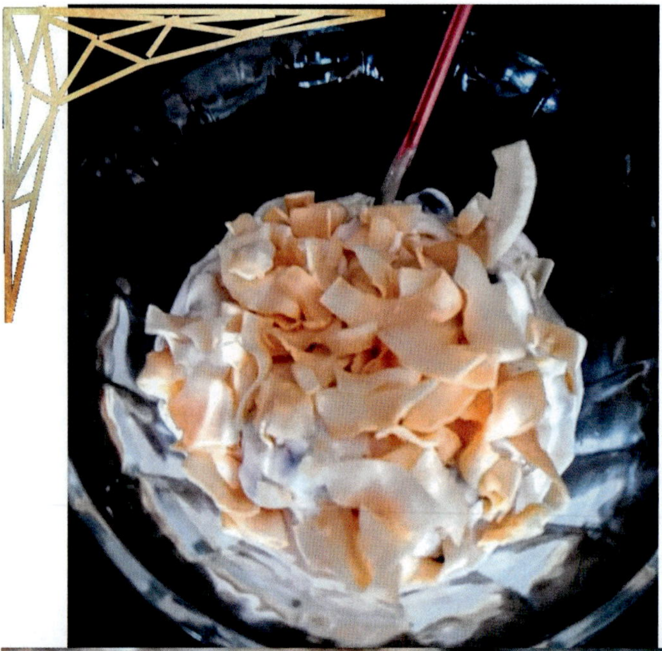
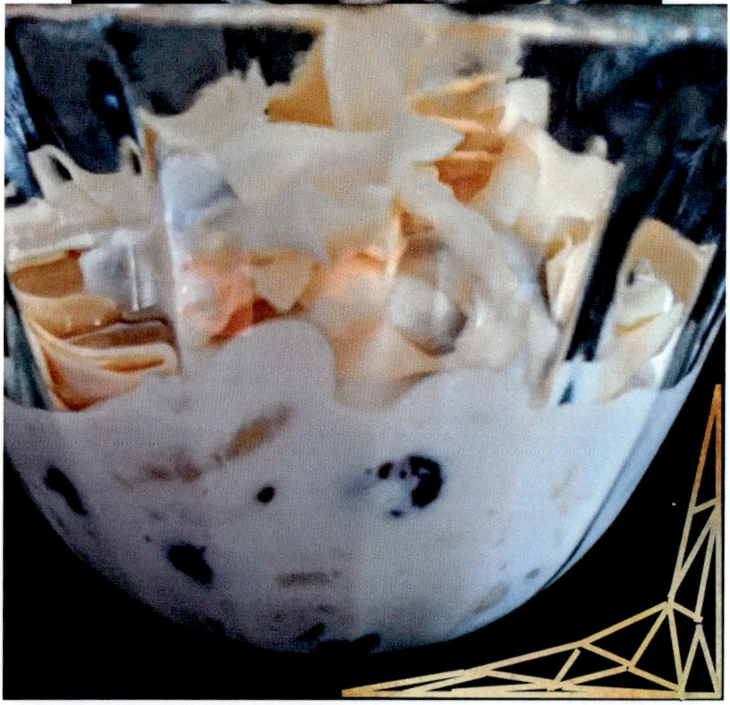

Toasted Coconut Limesicle

Ingredients:

6oz total: Banana, frozen pineapple, frozen blueberries (full fruit)

4oz Plain Greek yogurt (1/2 protein)

1oz Lime juice

1/2oz Toasted coconut (unsweetened coconut flakes work also) (full fat)

Directions: Mash banana. Add remaining frozen fruit, Greek yogurt, lime juice and mix. Top with coconut.

Side with 6oz vegetables and ½ protein for a complete lunch.

106

Tunamatoe Bites

Ingredients:

6oz Tomatoes (full vegetable)

1oz Tuna (1/4 protein)

2oz Plain Greek yogurt (1/4 protein)

1/2oz Mayo (full fat)

Pinch of each: Sea salt, pepper

1oz Cheese (1/2 protein)

2oz Pickles (condiment)

Directions: Slice tomatoes and pickles. In a separate bowl add tuna, Greek yogurt, mayo, seasonings, and mix. Top tomato slices with cheese, pickles, and tuna mixture.

Side with fruit for a complete lunch

Dinner

Dinner = 1 protein, 1 fat, and 14oz vegetables.

"But I want a slice too!!"

Have you ever been in a situation at a party, gathering or family event, they bring out the dessert and everyone is taking a slice? Then they come to offer you one, and you think to yourself, "I just want to have one with everyone else. Why can't I be "normal"? All my friends and family get to have one." But remember! We're learning to be thankful. You might be thinking, "I sure don't feel thankful. What do I have to be thankful for? When I do feel thankful, then I will be thankful." Here's my answer to that. Sometimes you have to fake it till you make it.

During this time of staying at home during the Covid-19 quarantine, most of us (if not all) have lived in our comfy sweats. After a while, I started to feel sluggish and fat, almost feeling like I wasn't losing weight! Then the day finally came where I had the opportunity to go out!! I was so excited!! I put on my pair of favorite skinny jeans and my favorite top, and I noticed that they fit a little baggier than the last time. I felt thinner, better, and even more energetic dressing up! It's the same way with thankfulness. It can be like a coat when your cold. You have to "put it on" and after a couple of minutes you start to warm up. This is why it's so important to remind ourselves what we are thankful for. Even the smallest things!

When we're in a situation where everyone else is having your favorite dessert, remind yourself, "I'm thankful to have a beautiful meal later. I'm thankful I get to have delicious cinnamon donuts for lunch and still lose weight. I'm thankful for spending time with family and not be ruled by food." You could go on and on and on and soon you will feel thankful and empowered to say "no".

Thankfulness isn't just a feeling. It's a choice. And that choice goes hand in hand with being content.

Phillipians 4:7-9 (MSG) *Before you know it, a sense of God's wholeness, everything coming together for good, will come and settle you down. It's wonderful what happens when Christ displaces worry at the center of your life. 8-9 Summing it all up, friends, I'd say you'll do best by filling your minds and meditating on things true, noble, reputable, authentic, compelling, gracious—the best, not the worst; the beautiful, not the ugly; things to praise, not things to curse. Put into practice what you learned from me, what you heard and saw and realized. Do that, and God, who makes everything work together, will work you into his most excellent harmonies.*

Phillippians 4:11-12 MSG *I don't have a sense of needing anything personally. I've learned by now to be quite content whatever my circumstances. I'm just as happy with little as with much, with much as with little. I've found the recipe for being happy whether full or hungry, hands full or hands empty. Whatever I have, wherever I am, I can make it through anything in the One who makes me who I am.*

The best recipe for happiness in life is being content! Being happy with what you have right at this moment. Not waiting to feel like it, but making the choice to be it. You do that by filling your mind with good things. Don't think about, "I can't have dessert. I can't have this or that. I don't get to join in. It's not fair." When you fill your mind with those things you become like this verse.

Philippians 3:18-19 (MSG) *Stick with me, friends. Keep track of those you see running this same course, headed for this same goal. There are many out there taking other paths, choosing other goals, and trying to get you to go along with them. I've warned you of them many times; sadly, I'm having to do it again. All they want is easy street. They hate Christ's Cross. But easy street is a dead-end street.* **Those who live there make their bellies their gods; belches are their praise; all they can think of is their appetites.**

When you are not content and filling your mind with thankfulness and good thoughts, you will be consumed by your appetite. If you really put it into perspective…it's just food! It has no lasting happiness. It has no eternal value to you. It's ONE PIECE OF FOOD. Is that piece of food more important than you're happiness? Then you're freedom? Then you're sanity? Then you're weight loss?

1 Timothy 6:6-9 *But godliness with contentment is great gain. ⁷ For we brought nothing into this world, and it is certain we can carry nothing out. ⁸ And having food and raiment let us be therewith content.*

Before you take that bite weigh the cost. Is that piece of food worth going through detox again? Is it worth the cravings that will come after? Is it worth the guilty feeling you will feel later? Is it worth your weight loss slowing or even stopping? Is it worth not reaching your goal? It's definitely not worth it to me. I don't want to serve food anymore. I'm making food serve me!

The easy definition of sin is doing something you know is wrong. And sin is very costly. It will take you farther than you want to go, keep you longer than you want to stay, and cost you more than you want to pay. You can't find contentment on easy street. It takes practice and thoughtfulness every day. But if you work at it, it will be the greatest thing you will learn! It's truly an amazing tool to get you to Deliciously Free! Let's learn how together!

Pray this with me. "Father God. I want to live a thankful and content life. Show me how I can do that. Remind me of all the things You have blessed me with in life. I trust You that You will never leave me without help and a way of escape in every situation. I give You my life. I give You my hopes and dreams. I know You have the best life in store for me, better than I could hope or even imagine. I trust You with my food. I trust You with my life. I trust You with my weight loss journey. Forgive me for not being thankful and complaining. Forgive me for always seeing the bad in situations. I choose to make thankfulness and being content a habit. I thank You for helping me learn to be Deliciously FREE! In Jesus Name, Amen."

With joy, Natalie

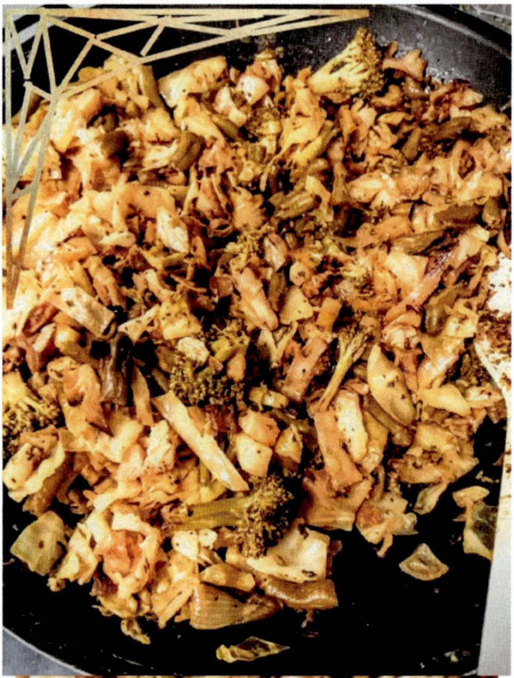

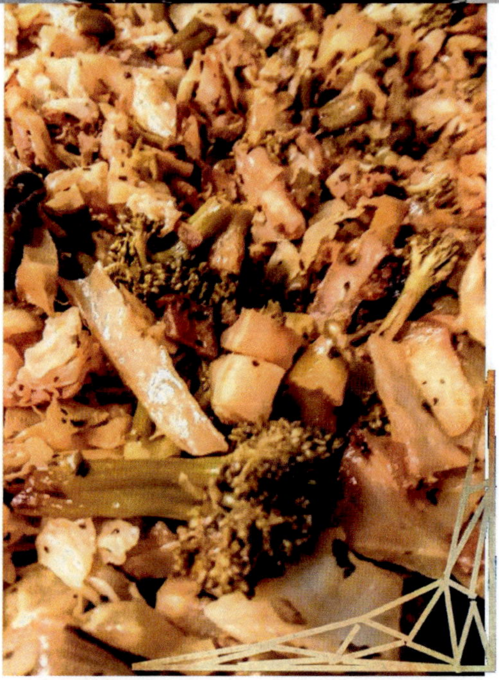

Asian Cabbage Stir Fry

Ingredients:

14oz total: Broccoli, onion, cabbage (full vegetable)

1Tbsp Toasted sesame oil (full fat)

Pinch of each: Ginger, onion powder, garlic salt, pepper

Directions: Heat and lightly oil a skillet, or wok. Chop vegetables. Add vegetables to skillet and cook 5-10min or until vegetables are tender. Add seasonings, toasted sesame oil and stir.

Side with a protein for a complete Dinner.

The Napa cabbage nice and crisp, it makes a perfect wrap

Avocado Egg Salad Wrap

Ingredients:

2oz Avocado (full fat)

1 Egg (1/2 protein)

7oz total: Napa cabbage leaves, onion, radish (1/2 vegetable)

1tsp Dijon mustard

Pinch of each: Sea salt, pepper, chives

2oz Pickled banana pepper (condiment 2oz free)

Directions: Chop avocado, egg, onion, and radish. Mix avocado, Dijon, salt, pepper, onion, and egg. Top cabbage leaves with radish slices. Scoop egg mixture on top and top with chives and banana peppers.

Side with 7oz vegetables for a complete dinner

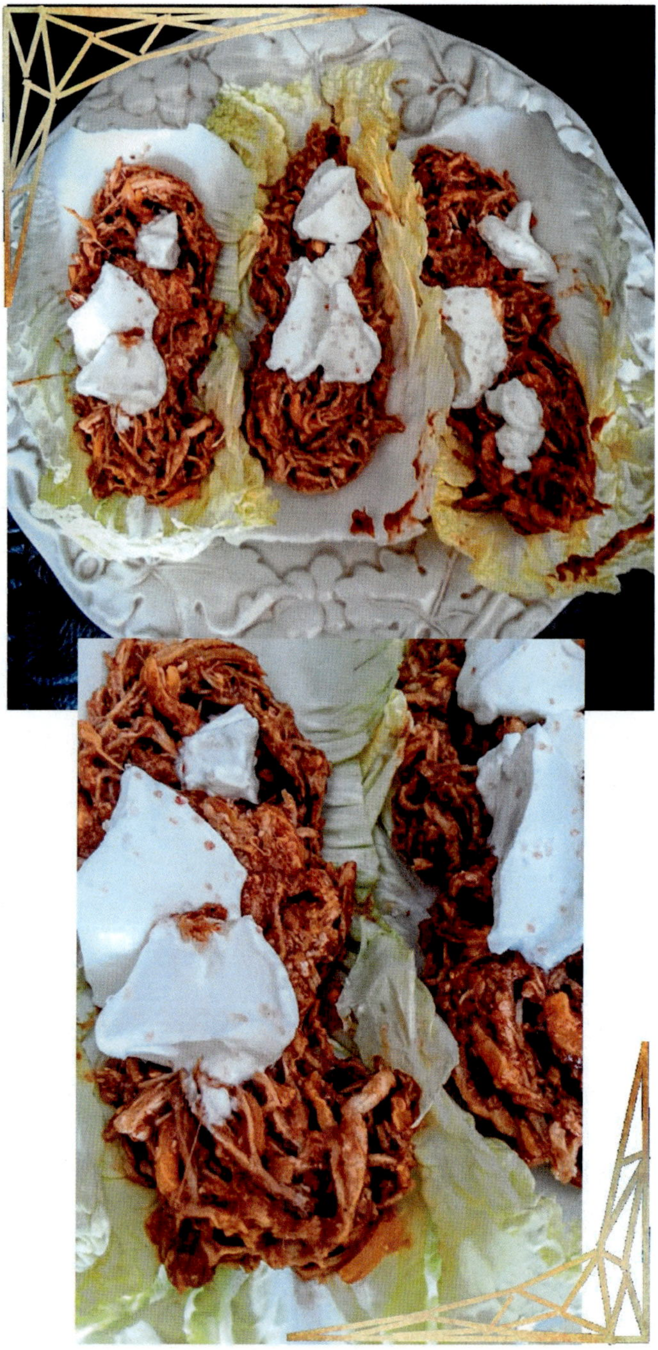

BBQ Chicken Wraps

Ingredients:

1oz Cheese (full fat)

3oz Cooked chicken (3/4 protein)

1oz Stubbs sugar free BBQ sauce (condiment)

7oz Napa cabbage (1/2 vegetable)

2oz Plain Greek yogurt (1/4 protein)

Directions: Add cheese, chicken, and BBQ sauce to a bowl and mix. Microwave mixture 1min. Spread mixture onto cabbage and top with Greek yogurt.

Side with 7oz vegetables for a complete dinner

Super easy, and super yummy dinner!

Slow Cooker Chicken Enchilada Soup

Ingredients:

14oz total: onion, 1 can diced tomatoes, yellow bell pepper (full vegetable)

2tsp of each: Cumin, oregano

2 Cloves garlic

Sea salt, pepper

8oz Vegetable broth (condiment 8oz free)

2oz Cooked chicken (1/2 protein)

2oz Avocado (full fat)

2oz Plain Greek yogurt (1/4 protein)

1/2oz Cheese (1/4 protein)

Directions: Dice onion and garlic. Sauté onion, garlic, and cumin. Add to a crockpot cooked onions, chicken, broth, tomatoes, oregano, salt, pepper, and peppers. Cook on high 5hrs. Top with remaining ingredients.

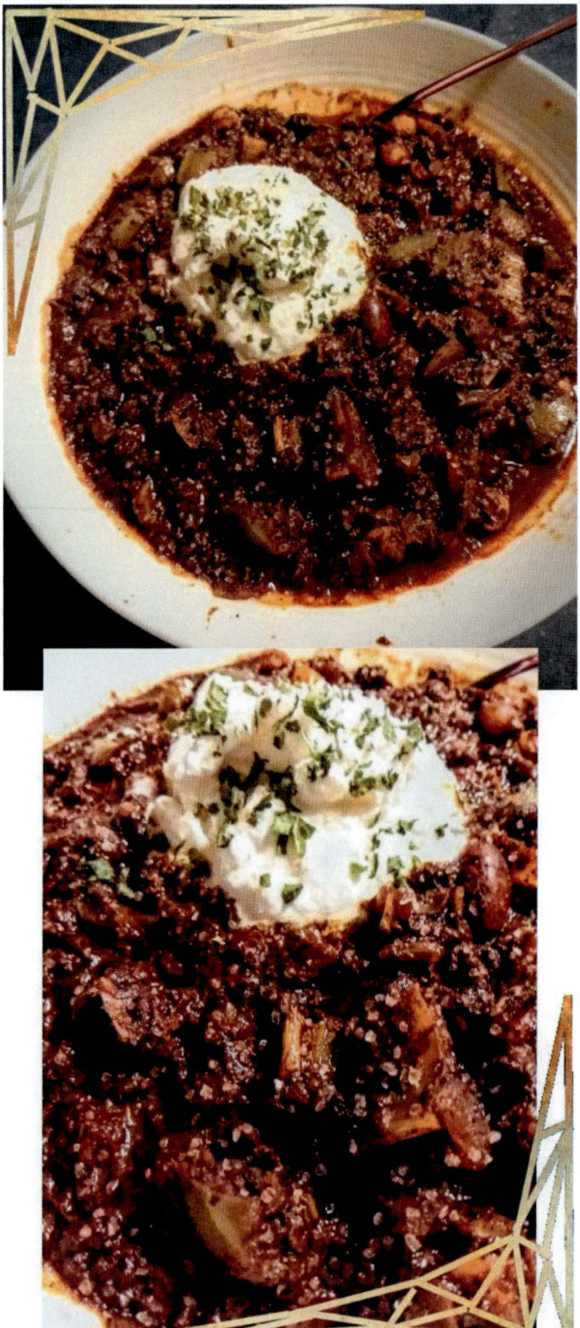

Chili

Ingredients:

14oz total: Onion, celery, green bell peppers, canned crushed tomatoes (full vegetable)

1 Bay leaf

1tsp Cumin

2Tbsp Oregano

Sea salt, pepper

3 Cloves garlic

1Tbsp Chili powder

4oz Vegetable broth (condiment up to 8oz free)

3oz total canned: Kidney beans, chickpeas, black beans (1/2 protein)

2oz Ground beef (1/2 protein)

2oz Ricotta cheese (full fat)

Directions: Brown ground beef. Dice/chop garlic, onion, peppers, and celery. Add onion, bay leaf, cumin, oregano, salt, and pepper to a large pot and sauté. Add peppers, celery, broth, and browned beef. Simmer 5min. Add tomatoes, chili powder, and beans. Bring to a boil, reduce heat to low. Simmer 45min. Remove bay leaf. Top with ricotta cheese.

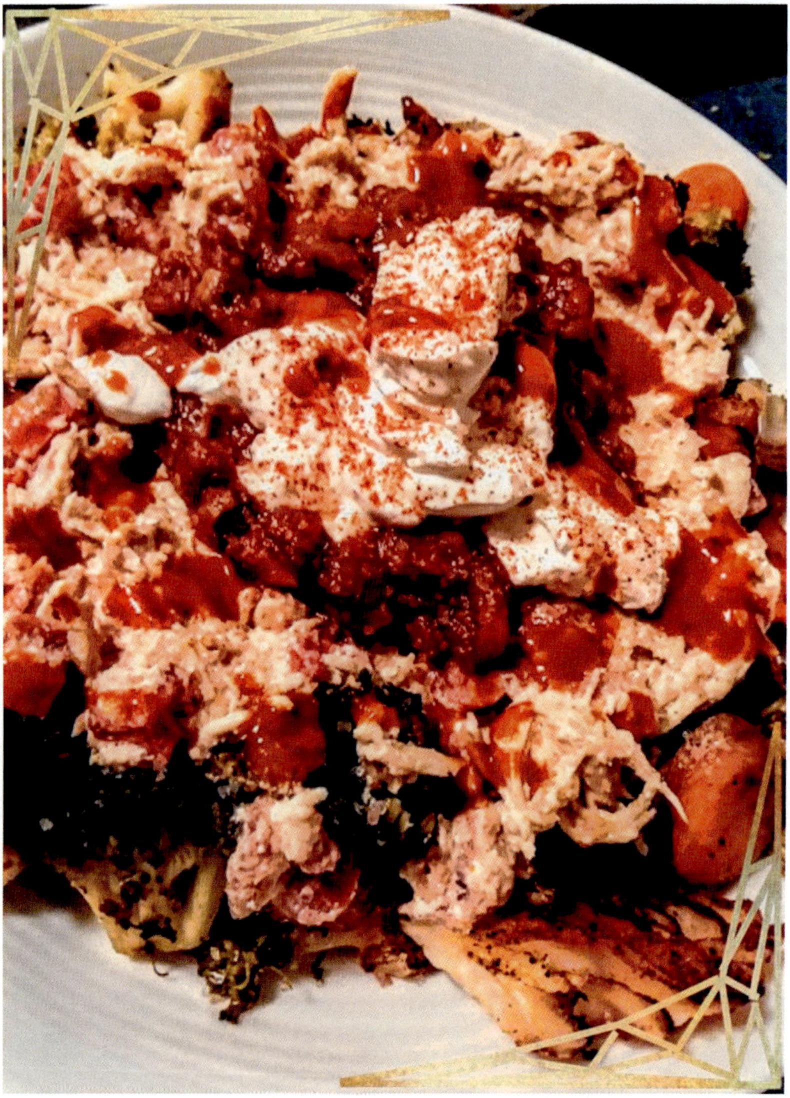

Creamy Taco Chicken Bowl

Ingredients:

3oz Taco chicken (3/4 protein)

2oz Ricotta cheese (full fat)

2oz Can Rotelle (condiment)

1oz Juice from can of Rotelle (condiment)

2oz Plain Greek yogurt (1/4 protein)

14oz total: Spring mix lettuce, onion, bell peppers, cucumber, tomato (full vegetable)

Hot sauce

2oz Salsa (condiment)

Pinch of Chipotle pepper powder

Directions: Add chicken, ricotta cheese, Rotelle and Rotelle juice to a bowl and mix. Microwave mixture 1min. Chop/dice vegetables and add to a large bowl. Top salad with creamy chicken mixture, Greek yogurt, hot sauce, salsa, and chipotle pepper powder.

The eggs in this dish taste like ravioli!

Eggs Pizzaiola

Ingredients:

2 Cloves garlic

Pinch of each: Sea salt, red pepper flakes, pepper, parsley, basil

2oz Vegetable broth (condiment up to 8oz free)

2oz Spaghetti sauce (condiment)

2 Eggs (full protein)

1oz Feta cheese (full fat)

2oz Spinach (subtract from dinner vegetable)

4oz Canned crushed tomatoes (subtract from dinner vegetable)

Directions: Dice garlic. Heat and lightly oil a small saucepan or pot. Sauté garlic until golden. Add seasonings, tomatoes, broth, spinach, spaghetti sauce, and bring to a boil. Reduce heat, add basil and simmer 5min. Gently crack eggs into pot and top with feta cheese. Cover and simmer on med/low 10-15min or until egg whites are cooked through.

Side with 8oz vegetables for a complete dinner.

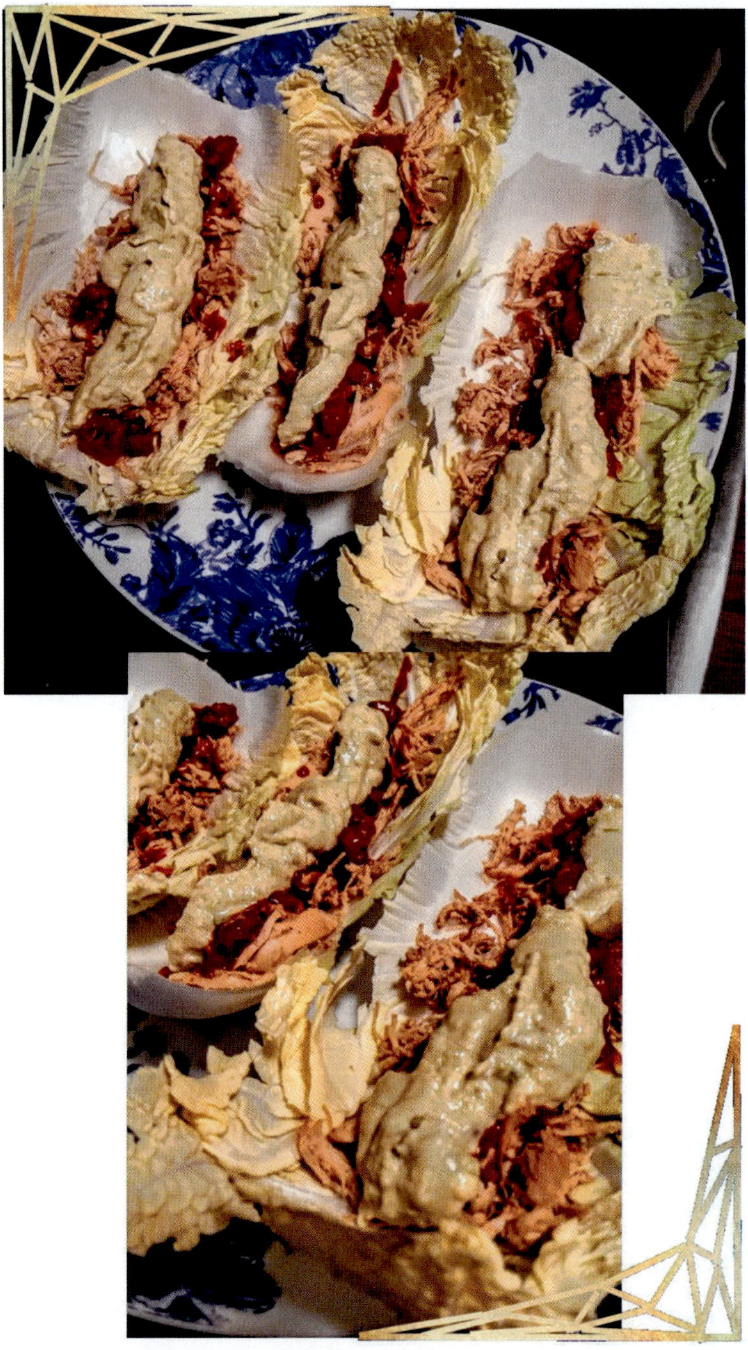

Cabbage Taco Wraps with Creamy Avocado Dressing

Ingredients:

7oz Napa cabbage (1/2 vegetable)

3oz Taco chicken (3/4 protein)

2oz Salsa (condiment)

Hot sauce

2oz Plain Greek yogurt (1/4 protein)

2oz Avocado (full fat)

1/2oz Lime juice

Directions: Top cabbage with taco chicken, salsa, and hot sauce. In a separate bowl add Greek yogurt, avocado, lime juice, splash of hot sauce and mash/mix. Top taco wraps with avocado dressing.

Side with 7oz vegetables for a complete dinner

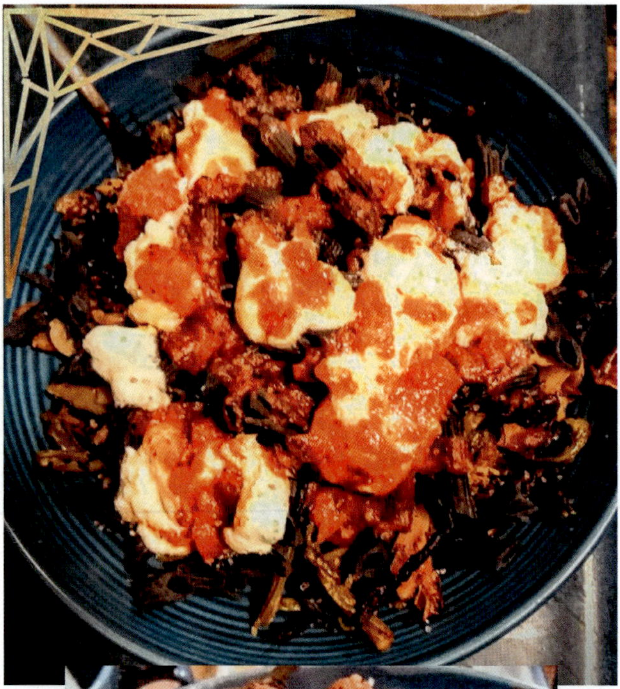

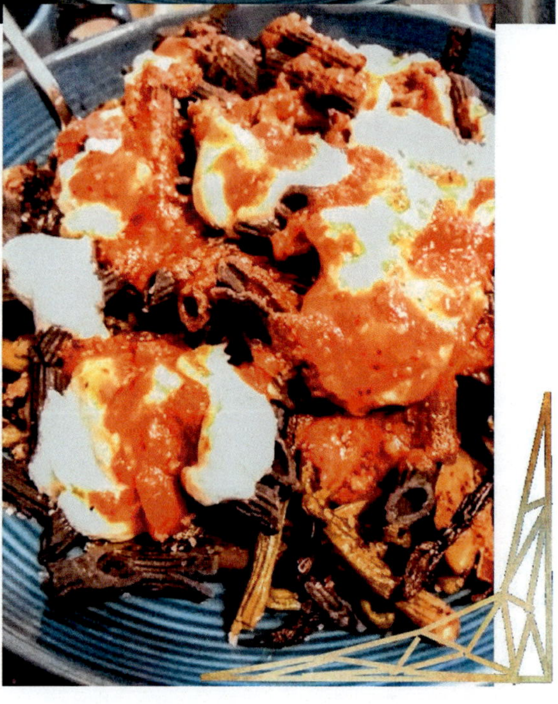

Veggie Lasagna Bowl

Ingredients:

3oz Black bean pasta (1/2 protein)

4oz Ricotta cheese (1/2 protein + full fat)

2oz Spaghetti sauce (condiment)

14oz Roasted vegetables (full vegetables)

Directions: Cook lentil pasta according to box directions. Roast vegetables. Layer vegetables, pasta, ricotta cheese and spaghetti sauce. (optional- Microwave 1-2min to heat cheese)

Make sure to check your pasta box label so it does not contain bean flour.

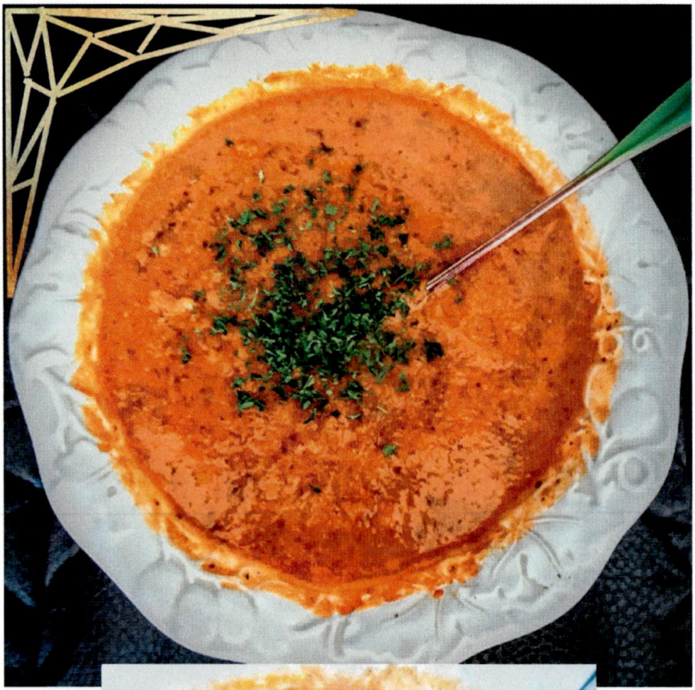

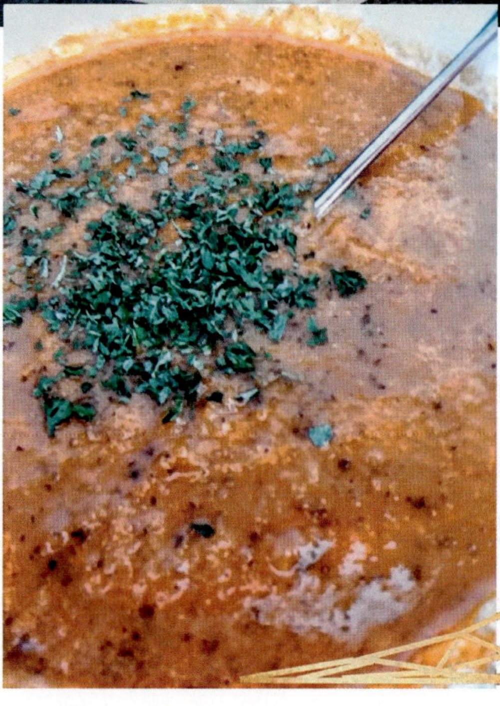

Sneaky Chickpea Soup

Ingredients:

3oz Canned chickpeas (1/2 pro)

1/2cup Aquafaba (condiment)

14oz total: Onion, celery, carrots, can diced tomato (full vegetable)

8oz Vegetable broth (condiment)

3 Cloves garlic

2oz Spaghetti sauce (condiment)

1tsp Oregano

2 Bay leaves

Sea salt

1Tbsp Basil

1oz Parmesan (1/2 pro)

Directions: Blend chickpeas and aquafaba. Dice vegetables. Sauté onion over medium heat 4-5min. Add garlic, celery, and carrots cook another 5min. Add broth, tomatoes, sauce, pureed chickpeas, and spices. Bring to a boil. Reduce heat, cover, and simmer 15min. Stirring occasionally. Remove bay leaves and blend soup. Simmer another 10min. Top with parmesan and more basil.

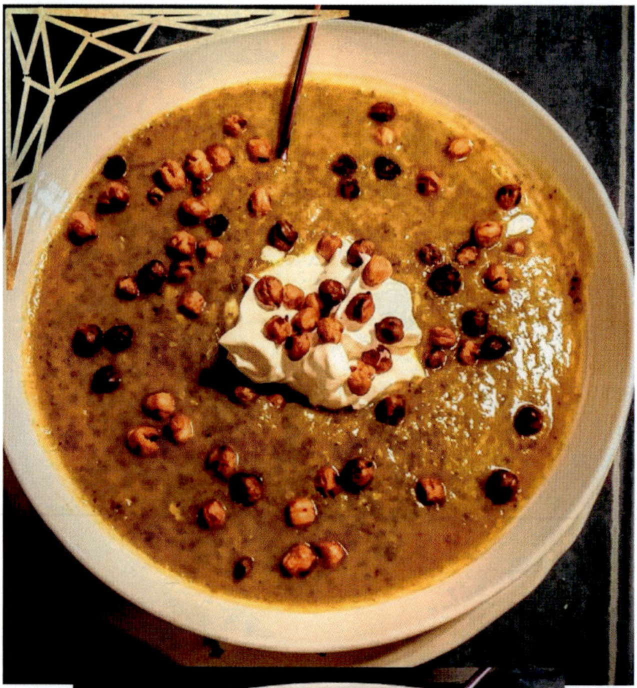

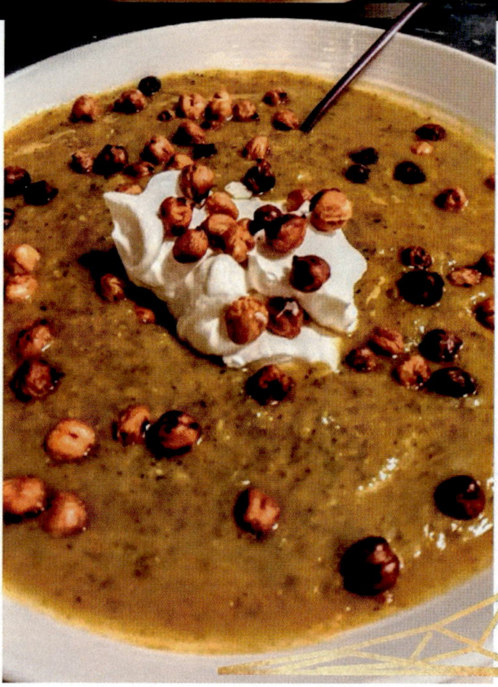

Cheesy Zucchini Soup

Ingredients:

14oz total: Onion, zucchini (full vegetable)

8oz Vegetable broth (condiment)

1oz Cheese (full fat)

Sea salt, pepper

1Tbsp Parsley

1tsp Garlic powder

1/4tsp Paprika

2oz Plain Greek yogurt (1/4 protein)

1oz *Roasted chickpeas (1/4 protein)

Directions: Sauté onions in coconut oil. Chop zucchini. Add zucchini and vegetable broth to onions and simmer. Partially cover pot with a lid and cook until zucchinis are fork tender. Remove pot from heat and stir in cheese. Use a hand blender to blend soup until smooth. Season with salt and pepper. Top with parsley and Greek yogurt and roasted chickpeas.

*Find Ranch Roasted Chickpeas in "Sauces, Seasonings, and Sides"
Side with ½ protein for a complete dinner.

Hot + cheesy = Delicious!

Cheesy Cauliflower Broccoli Bake

Ingredients:

14oz total: Frozen cauliflower, frozen broccoli (full vegetable)

Sea salt, pepper

3 Cloves garlic

2oz Milk (1/4 protein)

2oz Plain Greek yogurt (1/4 protein)

4oz Vegetable broth (condiment up to 8oz free)

1oz Cheese (full fat)

1oz Parmesan cheese (1/2 protein)

Directions: Preheat oven to 375. Dice garlic. Sauté garlic on med heat 1-2min in a medium pot. Add broth and milk. Bring to a boil. Remove from heat and stir in cheese and yogurt. In a separate large pot add cauliflower, broccoli, salt, and pepper. Sauté until vegetables are tender. Lightly grease a baking dish and add ½ of sauce, vegetables, and mix. Pour remaining sauce on top. Top with parmesan cheese. Cover and bake 20min. Remove cover and bake 5-15min until slightly golden.

Sauces, Seasonings, and Sides

Blueberry creamy dressing heaven!

Blueberry Coconut Vinaigrette

Ingredients:

2oz Full fat canned coconut milk (full fat)

1/2oz White wine vinegar

Splash of lemon juice

1oz Frozen blueberries (1/6 fruit)

Directions: Microwave blueberries 1min. Add remaining ingredients and mix.

Fat free dressing, so you can use as much as you like on your giant delicious salads!

Lemon Dijon Vinaigrette

Ingredients:

1oz Lemon juice

1 1/2oz White wine vinegar

1tsp Dijon mustard

Pinch of each: Basil, parsley

Directions: Add all ingredients to a container and mix. Store in fridge. Shake/stir before each use.

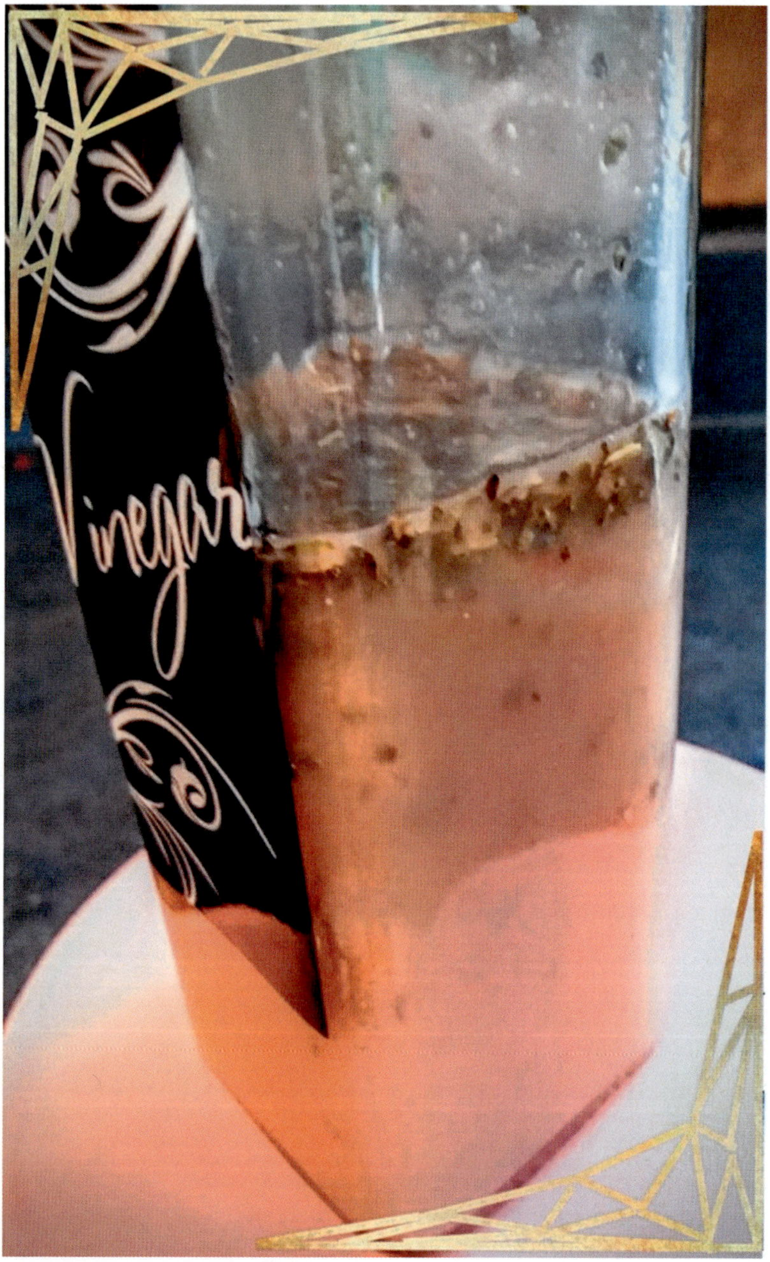
Vinegar

Red Wine Vinaigrette

Ingredients:

2oz Red wine vinegar

1oz Lemon juice

1tsp Dijon mustard

1/2tsp Basil

Pinch of Garlic salt

Directions: Add all ingredients to a container and mix. Store in fridge. Shake/stir before each use.

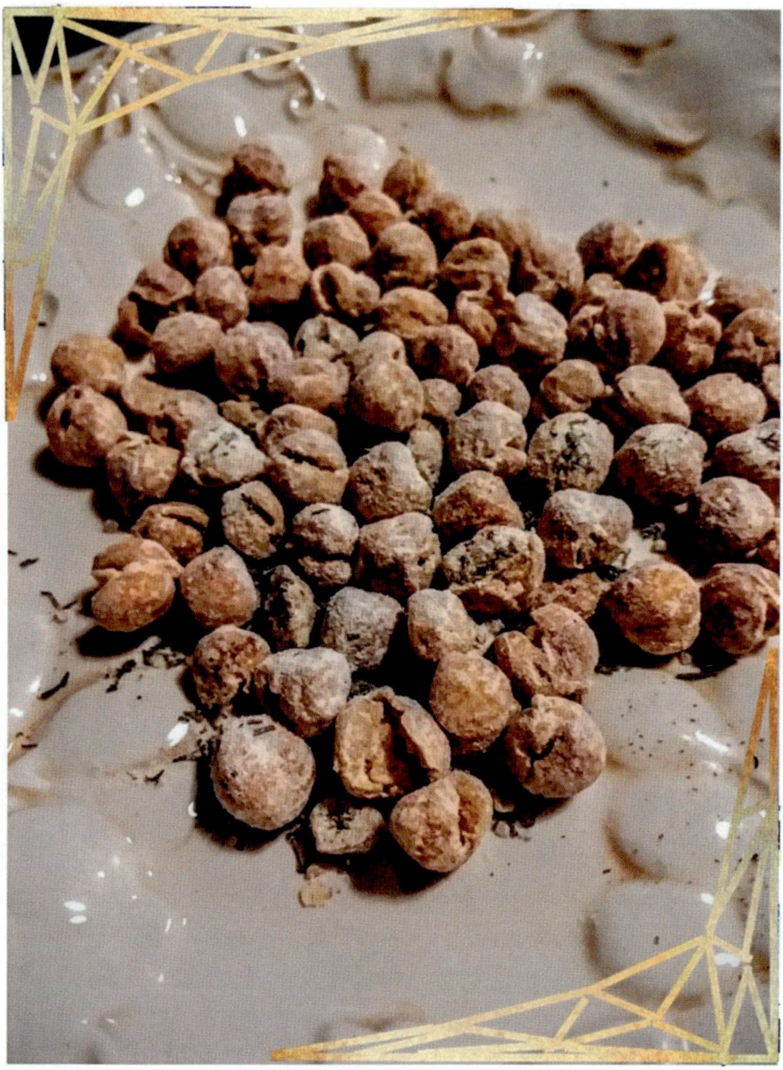

Ranch Roasted Chickpeas

Ingredients:

1 Can chickpeas

Olive oil

Pinch of each: Garlic powder, onion powder, dill, parsley

Sea salt

Directions: Preheat oven 450. Drain chickpeas and gently dry with a towel. Air dry until dry to the touch. Lightly coat with oil and cook 25min. shake pan halfway. turn oven off and leave beans in hot oven for 10min. Toss chickpeas in spices.

2oz = full protein

A little about me.

Growing up I never knew how normal healthy people ate. I have been overweight since I was about 9 years old. I always felt insecure about my weight and eating around others. Then as a family, we changed our diets to whole, healthy foods… and I still was over weight (it is possible to eat healthy foods and still be overweight). We never gave up our Friday night junk foods though.. Which slowly grew into Friday, Saturday junk food.. Then into all weekend junk foods.. And cravings all the rest of the week

As I grew up, I tried all the different kinds of diets with my mom and sister. They never lasted. The sugar and flour were always there… just waiting for us to fail… and we did. I even

tried the keto diet and lost 10 pounds! But…I went right back to the old eating habits.

Until one day, my mom called my sister and I into her room. She showed us the first video to an amazing plan on Facebook. It talked about how this way of eating takes all the willpower out. (Which is what we needed!!) We three girls started and went all out. Once we started, we quickly found out that this is the best lifestyle- ever!

After

For a couple of years, God had been speaking to my mom and He told her, "Your influence for Me will not be as effective in society if you remain overweight. People will be more accepting and open if you will lose the weight." (Sadly, our society is very judgmental) So that's what we did. This has been the best lifestyle change. (it is not a diet). I have lost over 80lbs and have never felt better! The body insecurities are GONE! I don't have to think, "What are they thinking about me. Do I look fat? Will I fit in that chair? I have to shop in the plus size section while all of my friends get to shop in the cute clothing sections." Now I can just throw on jeans and a t-shirt and I don't have to worry about my body or what I look like. I have so much energy. I don't have the tired headaches or the 'blec' feeling after eating junk food. I never have to feel insecure about eating food in front of other people. I can shop in the normal size people sections. I have never been this skinny in my whole life and I will never go back to the old me. Never! I'm not at my goal weight yet but I'm enjoying the journey. It is truly Happy, Healthy, Skinny, and Free!!

With joy, Natalie

About the Author

Natalie was born and raised in Minnesota and was home-schooled along with her siblings. She works full-time with her family at Love of God Family Church in Fergus Falls, Minnesota, leading worship, singing, playing keyboard, and drums. She also writes skits and performs with the church's Blast Kids program. She is also the founder and creator of Closet Critters.

If you would like more information about Bright Line Eating (which I 100% recommend!) you can go to https://brightlineeating.com. I started with the 14-day challenge and it was fantastic, and very reasonably priced, or order the Bright Line Eating book.

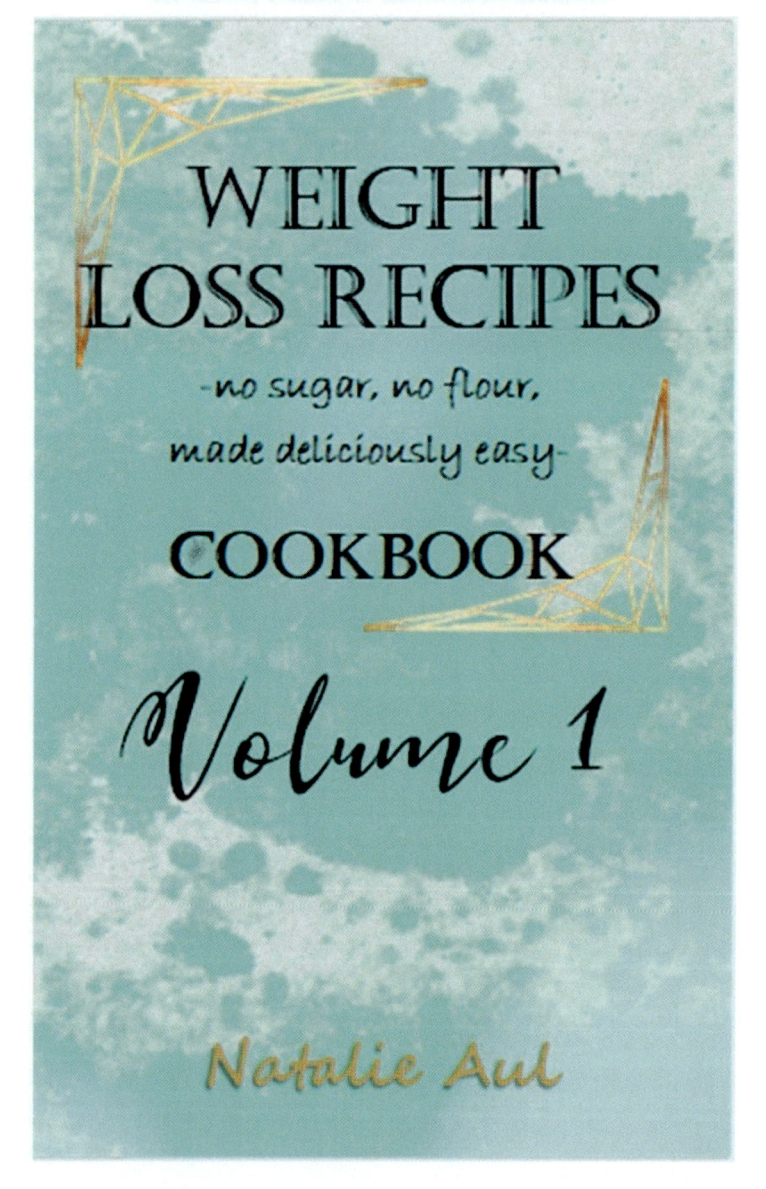

60 BRAND NEW RECIPES IN VOLUME ONE!
ORDER YOURS TODAY!
WeightLossRecipesCookbook.com
Or visit Barnes & Noble online

WEIGHT LOSS RECIPES

-no sugar, no flour, made deliciously easy-

COOKBOOK

Volume 1

Natalie Aul

60 BRAND NEW RECIPES IN VOLUME TWO!
ORDER YOURS TODAY!
WeightLossRecipesCookbook.com
Or visit Barnes & Noble online

WEIGHT LOSS RECIPES

-no sugar, no flour, made deliciously easy-

COOKBOOK

Volume 2

Natalie Aul

**60 BRAND NEW RECIPES IN VOLUME THREE!
ORDER YOURS TODAY!**
WeightLossRecipesCookbook.com
Or visit Barnes & Noble online

WEIGHT LOSS RECIPES

-no sugar, no flour, made deliciously easy-

COOKBOOK

Volume 3

Natalie Aul

60 BRAND NEW RECIPES IN VOLUME FOUR!
ORDER YOURS TODAY!
WeightLossRecipesCookbook.com
Or visit Barnes & Noble online

WEIGHT LOSS RECIPES

-no sugar, no flour, made deliciously easy-

COOKBOOK

Volume 4

Natalie Aul

60 BRAND NEW RECIPES IN VOLUME FIVE!
ORDER YOURS TODAY!
WeightLossRecipesCookbook.com
Or visit Barnes & Noble online

WEIGHT LOSS RECIPES

-no sugar, no flour, made deliciously easy-

COOKBOOK

Volume 5

Natalie Aul

**60 BRAND NEW RECIPES IN VOLUME SIX!
ORDER YOURS TODAY!
WeightLossRecipesCookbook.com
Or visit Barnes & Noble online**

WEIGHT LOSS RECIPES

-no sugar, no flour, made deliciously easy-

COOKBOOK

Volume 6

Natalie Aul

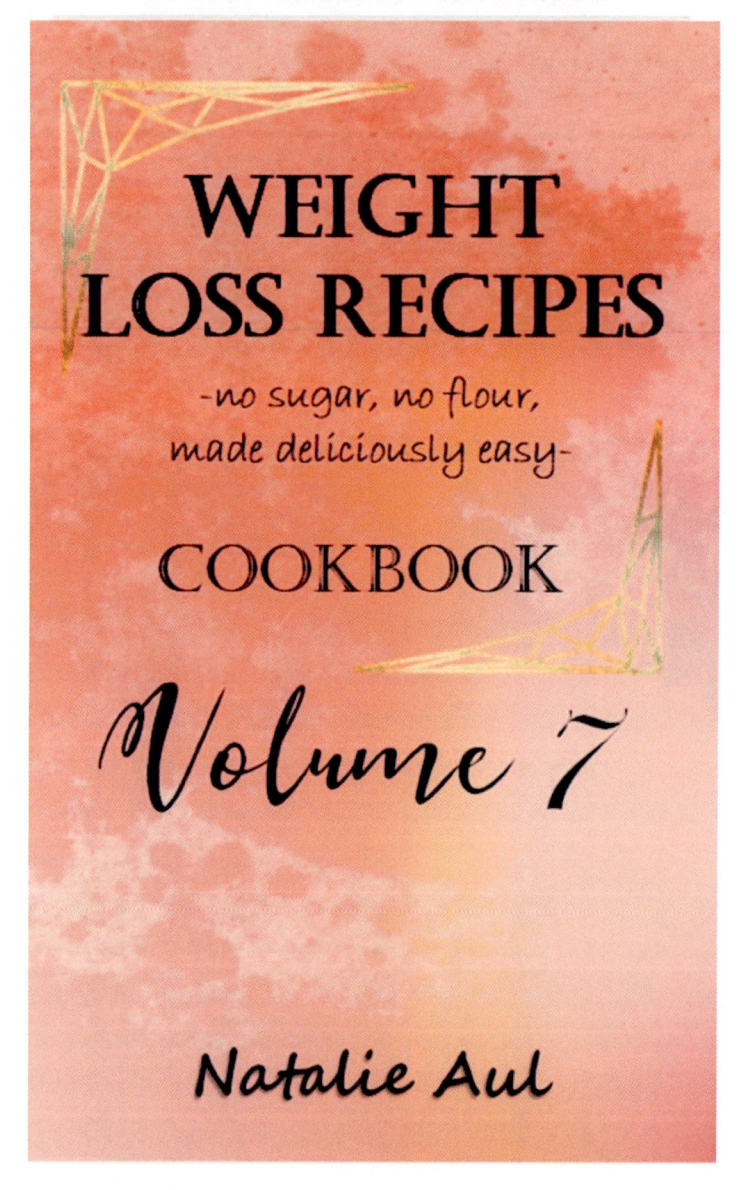

**60 BRAND NEW RECIPES IN VOLUME SEVEN!
ORDER YOURS TODAY!
WeightLossRecipesCookbook.com
Or visit Barnes & Noble online**

WEIGHT LOSS RECIPES

-no sugar, no flour, made deliciously easy-

COOKBOOK

Volume 7

Natalie Aul

Volumes 1-5 in one BIG BOOK! Over 300 recipes in one. You will love Cooking with Joy. Order yours today!

WeightLossRecipesCookbook.com

Or visit Barnes & Noble online

60 Delicious recipes with all of the Whole Food, Plant Based, and Vegan recipes from volumes 1-5 in 1 cookbook.

WeightLossRecipesCookbook.com

Or visit Barnes & Noble online

WEIGHT LOSS RECIPES

-no sugar, no flour, made deliciously easy-

COOKBOOK

Whole Food, Plant Based, & Vegan Volume

Natalie Aul

THIS VOLUME CONTAINS 14 DAYS OF BREAKFAST, LUNCH, AND DINNER, TO GET YOU STARTED IN THE RIGHT DIRECTION.

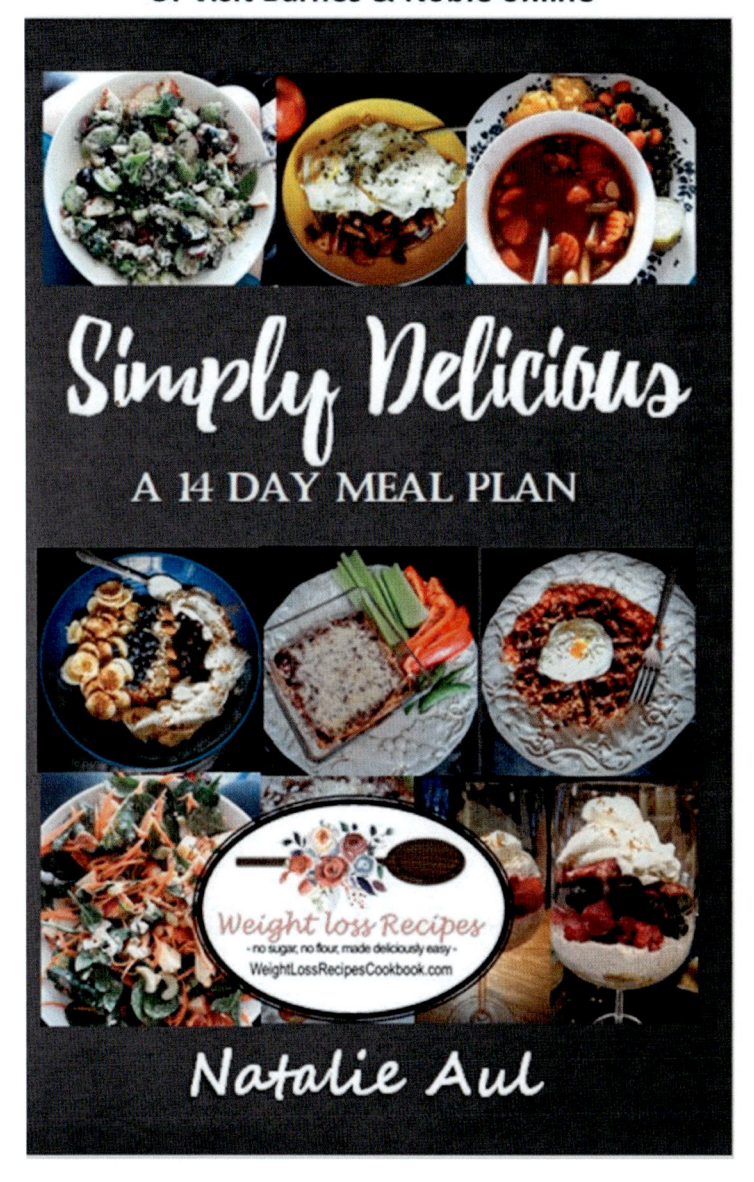

WeightLossRecipesCookbook.com

Or visit Barnes & Noble online

Simply Delicious
A 14 DAY MEAL PLAN

Weight Loss Recipes
- no sugar, no flour, made deliciously easy -
WeightLossRecipesCookbook.com

Natalie Aul

Finally, an affordable product everyone can use!

Our Products

We sell all natural skin and body care products with no artificial, synthetic, or GMO's. Just the very basic, wholesome ingredients you can trust.

About Our Products

We found it hard to find natural products that were actually affordable so we began to make our own products that contain very few ingredients. We found pure freedom in these products. Not only free from harmful chemicals and ingredients that we can't even pronounce but also free from the financial stress of trying to find natural products that fit into our budget.

The natural ingredients in our products are simple, basic, and essential. This simplicity and peace of mind gives you PURE FREEDOM

AULNATURAL.COM

aulnatural@yahoo.com - FACEBOOK.COM/AulNatural

218-685-4507

Christian Historical Romance Fiction Novels by
Kelly Aul

These books capture the hearts of all ages with inspiring stories filled with adventure, romance, thrilling twists, and hope. Most importantly, they are pure and appropriate for everyone.

Available in Stores:
Trumm Drug in Elbow Lake, MN
Higher Grounds in Fergus Falls, MN

Available Online:
Amazon (ebook and paperback)
Barnes & Noble (ebook and hardcover)

Never Forsaken Series
1. Audrey's Sunrise
2. In the Midst of Darkness
3. Holding Faith
4. Everlasting

Relentless Series
1. Unspoken Pursuit

www.KellyAul.com

Facebook.com/
KellyAulNovels

Purebooks
"Blessed are the pure in heart for they shall see God."
Matthew 5:8

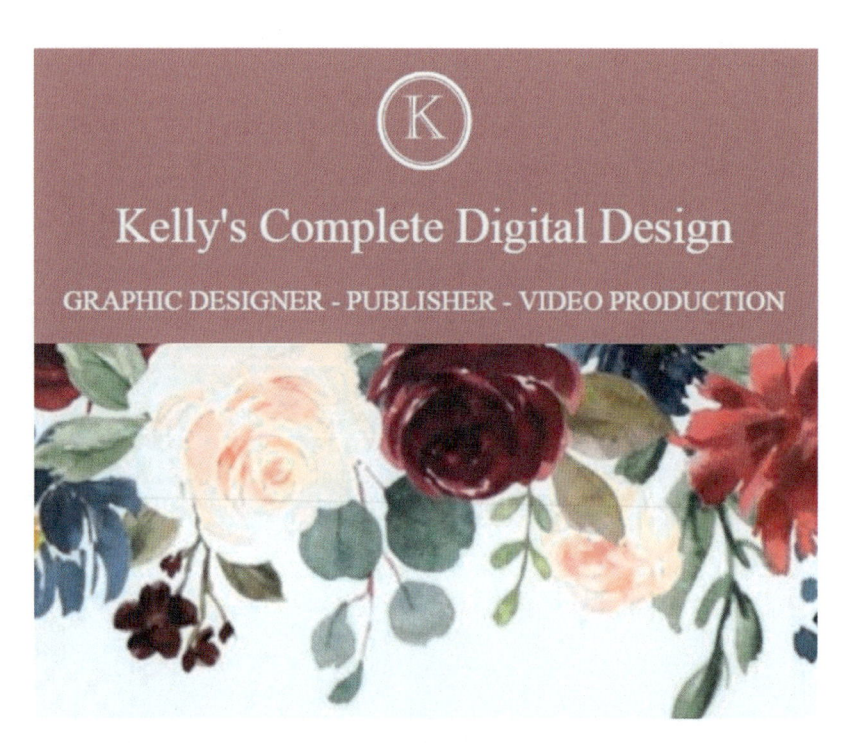

Kelly's Complete Digital Design

GRAPHIC DESIGNER - PUBLISHER - VIDEO PRODUCTION

WHETHER YOU ARE A CHURCH, COMPANY, SMALL BUSINESS, OR WANT TO PUBLISH YOUR WORK, I WOULD LIKE TO HELP YOU, ALL THE WHILE KEEPING IT LOW COST AND AFFORDABLE. I WANT TO MAKE THE ENTIRE PROCESS AS EASY AND SIMPLE AS POSSIBLE. PLEASE CONTACT ME TODAY FOR A CONSULTATION AND QUOTE FOR WHAT YOU ARE LOOKING FOR. I LOOK FORWARD TO HELPING YOU.
KELLY

KELLYAULNOVELS.COM

FACEBOOK.COM/ KELLYAULNOVELS

PUBLISHER

Have you written a poem, children's book, or novel but don't know how to share it with the world? Let me help! I will work with you in creating a unique and professional looking book, without it costing a fortune.

- **PUBLISH ON AMAZON BARNES & NOBLE**
- **BOOK COVERS**
- **FORMATTING**
- **EDITING**
- **EBOOKS**
- **PAPERPACK BOOKS**
- **HARDCOVER BOOKS**
- **ISBN NUMBERS**
- **EIN TAX ID NUMBERS**

GRAPHIC DESIGNER

Let me help you in all of your advertising needs, whether it's a fun event or a new business venture. I will work with you to create affordable designs that will catch everyone's eye and make a lasting impression.

- **LOGOS**
- **FLYERS**
- **BUSINESS CARDS**
- **NEWSLETTERS**
- **MAGAZINES**
- **BROCHURES**
- **COVER LETTERS**
- **POWERPOINTS**
- **PHOTO EDITING**
- **DVD/CD COVERS**
- **BASIC WEBSITE DESIGNER**
- **FACEBOOK COVER PHOTOS**
- **SOCIAL MEDIA MANAGER**

VIDEO PRODUCTION

⚙

Let me help you make affordable, memorable videos that capture life's priceless moments and will last for generations.

- **GRADUATION VIDEOS**
- **WEDDING VIDEOS**
- **MEMORIAL VIDEOS**
- **SLIDESHOWS**
- **VIDEO INTRO / OUTRO**
- **ADVERTISEMENT VIDEOS**
- **VIDEOS LOOPS**
- **INSTRUCTIONAL VIDEOS**
- **VHS TO DVD TRANSFER**

Love of God Family Church

Loving God
His Word, His People

It's like coming home...

We're a family growing together in worship. We serve, laugh, play games, learn, and we share one another's victories and sorrows.

Our doors are open. Our hearts are open, also. If you're looking for a place to belong and grow close to God,

Welcome home!

Pastors Tom & Maggie Aul

www.LoveofGodFamilyChurch.com

Sunday Service   (LIVE STREAM ON FACEBOOK)
11:00am – 829 N. Tower Road, Fergus Falls, MN
Sunday Radio Program
7:30am KBRF 12.50 AM
Fergus Falls P.E.G. ACCESS TV
Sundays at 4:00pm / Mondays at 7:00pm / Fridays at 7:00am
First Sunday of Each Month
Food and fellowship after the service
The Sunday of Each Month after TAYA
(during the school year)
Service will be at 4:00pm
Tuesdays   (LIVE STREAM ON FACEBOOK)
Prayer - 5:30-6:30pm / Bible Study - 6:30-7:30pm
Wednesday Nights (LIVE STREAM ON FACEBOOK)
"BLAST" (Bible Learning And Seeking Truth) Kids Night
6:00-7:00pm for ages 3 and up—Free and free bus ride
Second Saturday of Each Month:
Gals Bible Study / 2:00-4:00pm
Guys Bible Study / 2:00-4:00pm
Third Saturday of Each Month:
TAYA (Teens And Young Adults) Games Night
YMCA in Fergus Falls, MN   - Free bus ride
6:30-10:00pm / For ages 9-25 / $4.00 to come
Forth Friday of Each Month:
TAYA FOR REAL
Free and free food, prizes, and bus ride
7:00-8:30pm / For ages 9-25
Exercise Classes
Tuesdays — Zumba 4:00pm, Bone Strengthening Exercise 4:30pm

Purebooks

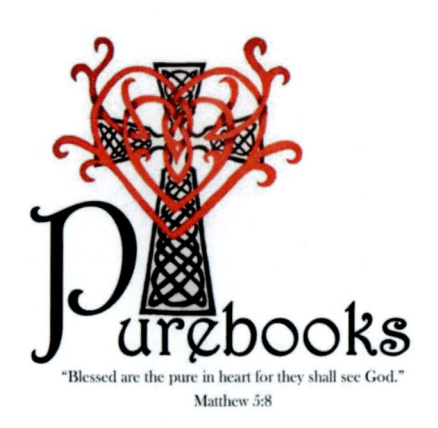

"Blessed are the pure in heart for they shall see God."
Matthew 5:8

This book was published by Purebooks Publishing Company which is a part of Kelly's Complete Digital Design.

KELLYAULNOVELS.COM

Manufactured by Amazon.ca
Bolton, ON